County Council

Libraries, books and more.........

I   of the
ju   etition,
ru   e clear
w   otional
tr   ith the
qu   th him,
ar   e book.
I   e since
w   ished I
re   y what
D   teaches
c   a book
a   ould be
i   -telling.
I   tension
a   for the
r   d never
e   *he Perfect*

Pair is now a key   .ules that I teach at the
University of Sal

This year, I in   guest lecture to our first
year writing students. The cla   nd many of our students
were inspired, not only to try out the great writing techniques that they
were shown, but also to take a wider interest in the issues that the book

raises. So it was with great anticipation that I awaited the manuscript of this second volume, *The Perfect Pair: The Mirror Cracks*. I was not disappointed. After reading into the early hours, I finished with a yelp of frustration because I was going to have to wait for the third volume to find out what happens to these utterly compelling characters, both animal and human. Not surprisingly, this volume has a darker tone as our young hero and his dolphins grow up, learning to navigate the cynical financial interests that dictate the conditions of their existence. But there are also moments of humour and triumph as this idealistic young man risks body and soul to protect his beloved charges. This narrative has the richness, the light and shade, that makes for a deeply satisfying read.

I am all too familiar with the slings and arrows of trying to get things published, but I've never before seen difficulties of the magnitude that David and Tracy have encountered in bringing their work to print. So my message to you, the reader, is: spread the word! If you've enjoyed this book, tell others about it, give copies as presents, post reviews on-line. Let's get this story the audience it deserves.

Dr Ursula Hurley, MA Cantab, MA Lancaster, Fellow of the Higher Education Academy
Senior Lecturer in English and Creative Writing at the University of Salford

★★★

Part two of *The Perfect Pair* sees the aquatic circus world turn mammal asylum as the ringmasters of capitalism pull the profit strings even tighter around the psyches of both man and dolphins.

The cruel world of performing pool animals gets even madder with a gangster dolphin bullying his captive companions, taking on his trainer and deliberately flashing his, er, dolphinhood at little girls in the audience. Meanwhile, a female dolphin attempts to seduce her trainer, as her intended dolphin mate gets his sex kicks from a plastic penguin. Not so much Flippa as everyone's flipped. Not so much *The Mirror Cracks* as everyone cracks up.

It all takes place in the filthy, murky, sleazy, unfiltered waters of a corporate dolphinarium that's a metaphor for the filthy, murky, sleazy, unfiltered waters of big business where money rules the waves of humanity.

It's sad, it's mad and the gangster dolphin's b-a-a-a-d but it makes you want to dive into every page to keep reading what weirdness will happen next behind the scenes of the freak show that passes for aquatic entertainment.

Get the first brilliant book, *The Perfect Pair: The Enchanted Mirror*, then experience this sensational sequel. I guarantee you'll gobble it up like a dolphin showered with reward fish… and be clapping like a sea lion for more…

Stephen Kingston
Editor, *Salford Star*

★★★

As an animal lover, I feel the love. As a psychic, I feel the *connection*. As a human being, I feel that The Universe demands this story be told!

Please read… this is the book of the century.

Spirit Guide Cara
Psychic to the Stars

★★★

David and Tracy… brilliant! I was immediately drawn in by this book, written with such clarity and depth of feeling that I became one with David Capello, experiencing both his highs and his lows. An amazing book once again leaving me desperate to read and know more. Thanks for sharing this with me and all the other lucky readers!

Jill Bowyer
Radio Presenter

★★★

In the first volume, *The Perfect Pair: The Enchanted Mirror*, the authors introduce us to the exciting show biz world of the commercial dolphinarium. Capello, the new apprentice, enters the amazingly intense environment of dolphin training and quickly develops a natural understanding and empathy for these intelligent mammals.

Dolphins arguably have one of the most advanced communication abilities in the animal kingdom, and the intensity of this shocks him. In this second volume, *The Perfect Pair: The Mirror Cracks*, his special gift gradually enlightens him to their plight. He realises that limiting these magnificent creatures into a confined, barren and captive environment utterly compromises their welfare. In fact, his close relationship with his super-intelligent dolphins is all the environmental enrichment they have to live for.

The real tragedy is that if the public could actually see the plight behind the dolphin smile, they would no longer support this kind of show. At last! David and Tracy have given the public an opportunity to understand this in a beautifully written story.

I hope everyone will read it.

Simon JR Adams, BSc, BVMS, MRCVS
Zoo & Wildlife Veterinary Adviser

★★★

Beautifully revealed by gifted wordsmiths, David and Tracy, this previously untold story of a young man with a passionate love for his *Perfect Pair*, Duchess and Herb'e, continues to unravel. On one side, he faces increasingly unhealthy conditions and changing situations imposed by the management hierarchy and, on the other, experiences the deeper realms of dolphin nature in a battle of wills with the devious Clyde! A young man dealing with insurmountable pressures almost alone... but for that wonderful and powerful bond with his dolphins.

The second part of this enthralling story brings us an important lesson from history! You will be eagerly waiting to read the final part of this trilogy!

Very well done, David and Tracy – much love and support to you both.

Ian Rothwell
Radio Presenter

★★★

In this book, the sequel to *The Perfect Pair: The Enchanted Mirror*, we hear of the continued excitement, hard work and telepathy between dolphins and trainer whilst trying to perfect tricks for the entertainment of the public.

Each dolphin has its own personality and emotions – love, jealousy and hate – creating difficulties in their relationships and, interestingly, mirroring human behaviour.

David Capello's whole life was devoted to these delightful animals, but the captive conditions in which they lived became of great concern to him, eventually affecting his own health.

The author's engaging style of writing not only conveys the sad aspects of this story, but the hilarious ones as well. You'll find yourself laughing – usually at Capello's expense!

A very good read.

Sheila Reeves Rigby
Author of *Life's Mysteries – Your Key to Understanding*

★★★

Following hot on the heels of the first instalment, the brilliant *The Perfect Pair: The Enchanted Mirror*, this book, *The Perfect Pair: The Mirror Cracks*, does not disappoint in the least.

Poised on a knife-edge, the reader eagerly awaits the unfolding of this mystical story about a young man and his beloved dolphins. A tinge of doom lurks in our peripheral vision: we know it's coming and we patiently wait for it to announce its arrival.

The story exposes the dark and sinister side of the dolphin entertainment industry. Beneath the startling crystal blue of the dolphin tank, we learn of dolphins starved and tortured endlessly until they become mangled, twisted versions of an ocean clown… all at the behest of merciless money-hungry CEOs.

We learn how the welfare of the animals comes second to the ocean park's profit margins. Critical decisions are based on money alone and the animals are clearly not the focus of the park, but rather a means to an end…

As we learn of these atrocities, we are at the same time drawn further into the minds of the trainer and his dolphins, and their *connection* leaves you spellbound.

It is our hope that whoever reads this book will feel compelled to change their mindset and engage with its contents. It is high time that all animal entertainment industries be forced to answer critical questions and realize that, in the 21st century, mankind should not be inflicting pain, stress and unnatural habitats on clever, sentient beings.

Surely as the dominant species on this Earth, we can understand the inhumanity of the captive industry?

An excellent sequel, which is both enlightening and engaging, and it comes highly recommended.

Jerusha and Bhavna Singh
Founders of the Facebook page Captivity Kills – Don't Buy a Ticket
www.facebook.com/CaptivityKillsDontBuyATicket

★★★

Deliver Us From Bobby!
Deliver Us From Bobby! is an original piece of life writing. It uses the outlandish device of a mal-contented Californian sea lion called Bobby to tell a story of male aggression and territoriality, as played out in a small mining town.

It is told in the first person and demonstrates the level of violence potentially unleashed over a contested parking place. This has the ring of truth as two men, our self-critical narrator being one, are ready to fight to the death over the spot.

The teller is even more culpable, having erased Bobby from his consciousness, so intent is he on combat. What ensues is as hilarious as it is serious. This wonderful piece of life has a beautiful ending, which suggests that a capacity for loyalty and empathy could be the flip side of male aggression.

Professor Brenda Cooper: Literary Critic
Commenting on David C Holroyd's winning entry for the *Manchester Evening News* Literary Competition – A Piece of Your Life 2011 (*Deliver Us from Bobby!* Chapter 11, *The Perfect Pair: The Enchanted Mirror*)

The Perfect Pair

The Mirror Cracks

David C Holroyd

and

Tracy J Holroyd

Matador
9 Priory Business Park
Kibworth Beauchamp
Leicestershire LE8 0RX, UK
Tel: (+44) 116 279 2299
Fax: (+44) 116 279 2277
Email: books@troubador.co.uk
Web: www.troubador.co.uk/matador

ISBN
SB: 978 1783062 775
HB: 978 1783062 782

British Library Cataloguing in Publication Data.
A catalogue record for this book is available from the British Library.

Printed and bound in the UK by TJ International, Padstow, Cornwall

Matador is an imprint of Troubador Publishing Ltd

FOREWORD FOR

By William Roache, MBE

From the very beginning of this second book in the dolphin trilogy, we are drawn into the mind of David on his intriguing and captivating quest for *The Perfect Pair*.

Not for one moment do you question the psychic *connection* – that two-way communication between David and his beloved dolphins. For this is indeed a love story. Why else would David tolerate the greed and cruelty of the men whose pursuit of money blinds them to the suffering of his dolphins?

The writing is superb and you share every moment of David's rollercoaster journey. The joy of the dolphins' achievements; the despair at Management's lack of care for their health; the problems with the staff; and, above all, the unrelenting stress and pressure of being solely responsible for the training and care of his precious charges.

But David's enthusiasm and determination drives everything forward and we too hold our breaths in anticipation of the making of *The Perfect Pair*.

I started to read this book and did not put it down until I'd finished. Not only is it a joy to read but it gives a fascinating and unique insight into the mind of the dolphin.

I congratulate David and Tracy on a wonderful read and I eagerly await the final book.

Further comment: "It deserves to be a best seller."

NOTES FROM THE AUTHORS

A huge 'thank you' to all you good people out there for staying with us on this watery rollercoaster. Your purchase of *The Perfect Pair: The Mirror Cracks*, the second book in the dolphin trilogy, is really appreciated, especially uplifting after what we've had to endure at the hands of certain nameless parties. It's staggering what lengths these shadowy figures will go to in the hope of stopping you, the public, from reading this story. So, boosted by your support, Tracy and I have decided to soldier on.

Unfortunately, due to the constant harassment and fear of legal ramifications, we are again forced to publish under the 'Fiction' banner and not 'Non-fiction', as we'd first intended. Even so, rest assured that all events chronicled within these pages did actually take place and can be authenticated by the original 'Flippa dolphin' records, long-since thought destroyed. Only the names of the people and places have been changed.

On a more defiant note, the names of the dolphins and animals remain intact. As Capello insists, "This isn't just my story, but also theirs..." He would not allow their existence to be questioned in any way.

As for the read itself, we are all very proud of this second book, which takes you even further into the secretive and often disturbing world of the late 60s/early 70s commercial dolphinarium. Yet, despite the dark undertone, we feel we've achieved this insight without being detrimental to the manuscript's true goal: the telling of the boundless love shared between a boy and his dolphins.

I truly believe that this book is unique – that there has never been another to take you so deeply into the minds of a trainer and his charges. Love or hate the aqua-circus, you will nonetheless find it impossible to resist the allure of 'the psychic trainer'.

So put all your prejudices aside and join with him as he transports you into the alien universe of the dolphin – a magical and thought-provoking experience that will leave you begging for more.

David C Holroyd

Throughout this manuscript, the troubled trainer, David Capello, repeatedly refers to how the world of people constantly disappoints him.

Well, join the club – it constantly disappoints me, too! Writing about the 1970s dolphinarium industry really brought home just how far some people were prepared to go to make a fast buck – a fact that is still relevant today.

Ask yourself, has anything really changed since those exploitative days of the 1970s?

Somehow, I think not.

The point I'm trying to make is that the story woven within the pages of *The Perfect Pair: The Mirror Cracks* is ageless and universal. No matter who suffers or who gets hurt, money, power and greed rule – an ethos that, sadly, will never change.

Yet this book also demonstrates another facet of the human condition: an enduring love that can survive even the greatest adversity.

So, before reading this book, close your eyes and mentally prepare.

Merge with the trainer…

… Immerse yourself in his world…

… Stand with him onstage as one being.

Only then will you experience the magic and intimacy that is known to but a privileged few.

When you've achieved this, you will understand.

See you on the other side.

Tracy J Holroyd

ACKNOWLEDGMENTS

We would like to thank the following people for all their help and support during the writing and production of this book:

Marion Ibbotson and Paul Goodier, who passionately shared our dreams, but never saw our project completed. We will always remember your love and support, and hope you enjoy this continuing read in Heaven.

Our fantastic Mum and Dad, Barbara and Ronnie Holroyd, who endured so much neglect during the writing of this book… please forgive!

William Roache, MBE, whose continued enthusiasm, celebrity and excellent forewords have helped propel us towards a wider audience.

Dr Ursula Hurley, MA Cantab, MA Lancaster, Fellow of the Higher Education Academy, Senior Lecturer in English and Creative Writing at the University of Salford for her ongoing support and fabulous endorsement.

Stephen Kingston, Editor, *Salford Star*, for his witty, insightful endorsement and terrific press coverage. (www.salfordstar.com)

Simon JR Adams, BSc, BVMS, MRCVS, Zoo & Wildlife Veterinary Adviser, for his continued encouragement, advice and endorsement. Also, for his unwavering belief in our project and his efforts to spread the word.

Spirit Guide Cara, Psychic to the Stars, for her boundless enthusiasm, friendship, spiritual guidance and magical endorsement.

Jill Bowyer for her endorsement and fun radio interviews – but especially for her friendship.

Sheila Reeves Rigby, author, for her valued feedback, warm encouragement and wonderful endorsement… and, more importantly, her continued friendship.

Jerusha and Bhavna Singh, Founders of the South African Facebook page *Captivity Kills – Don't Buy a Ticket* for their fabulous support in spreading our message and – more importantly – for highlighting the plight of captive animals worldwide. (www.facebook.com/CaptivityKillsDontBuyATicket)

Ian Rothwell for his endorsement, thought-provoking radio interviews and continued support and encouragement.

Our beloved cousin, Antony J Reid of Reid Design & Illustration (www.reiddesign.co.uk) for his advice and digital origination of the book's graphic layout. Not forgetting, once again, his delightful eccentricity and fabulous sense of humour!

Tony Flynn of SalfordOnline.com for his continuing support and excellent media coverage. (www.salfordonline.com)

The admins of the Facebook page *Open Your Left Eye* for their fantastic postings. (www.facebook.com/openyourlefteye)

Bernard Purrier, conservationist and educational speaker, for promoting our story.

Don and Irene Campbell for their ever-cheerful support and Don's marvellous photographs.

Shirley Swaine for her wonderful photographs; also, for permitting use of her father's phenomenal close-ups… thank you, too, Edgar Swaine.

Rosemary and Chris Lovett for their friendship, support and invaluable introduction to Simon.

Barbara and Vince Meehan for their input and friendship over the years.

Our dear cousins, Pamela and Albert Morris, for their constant support.

Our extended US family, Louise, David and Susan Rockstraw and Patricia and Annie Clark, who helped to pass the word Stateside.

Also in the USA, Frank Jones – fearless in his defence of animals and determined to spread our message.

Rodney James Charman for his cheerful support and spreading the word in Thailand.

Steve Suttie, former manager of Salford City Radio, for his vision in creating the 'Twisted Ear' drama production group, which started it all.

Georgina Dalton and Rowena Harding of Salix Homes Ltd, Salford for securing us welcome publicity.

Chris James Nicholson and Paul Ritson for their friendship and unwavering support.

Natalie Jane Peou for her faith in our message and her efforts to spread the word.

Terence David Joy, landlord of the Park Inn, Swinton, along with all his customers, for their interest and enthusiastic support.

Lenny Bowers, barman extraordinaire, for his sunny disposition and outstanding service.

The Park Inn's Thursday Night Snug Club, Joe Lillie, John Colpitts, Roger Collier and Tom Whiting, for their cheerful patience in the face of David's obsession.

Anita Mikolaites for her insightful and profound feedback, enthusiastic support and friendship.

Sandra Chapman and Pam Kaye for their friendship and loyalty over so many years.

Finally, the many friends and family members, too numerous to mention, who have supported and encouraged us. Thank you all: we love you.

CREDITS

Cover photograph of *The Perfect Pair* (spliced): Edgar Swaine and Don Campbell.

Cover design: Antony J Reid and David C Holroyd.

Cover font: *The Perfect Pair* – created and designed by David C Holroyd.

Digital origination of the book's graphic layout and artwork: Antony J Reid of Reid Design & Illustration. www.reiddesign.co.uk

Original photographs: Don Campbell, Vince Meehan, Shirley Swaine, Edgar Swaine and David C Holroyd.

Digital restoration of original photographs: Tracy J Holroyd.

Line drawings (badge artwork): David C Holroyd.

❦ PROLOGUE ❧

"And now, ladies and gentleman, it's time for Duchess' highball, the only trick that Duchess performs alone. Normally, as you've already seen, she works as a team with Flippa. Now, at twenty-three feet, this is the highest highball in the country – an exceptional achievement for Duchess – so, if you have cameras, this is the time to use them. If you want a real good shot, you're welcome to come down to the front of the dolphinarium. All I ask is that once the trick is performed, you go straight back to your seats. Oh, and, by the way, you could get very wet. You have been warned."

Good old Dan, he's really giving Duchess' highball a big build-up, milking the trick for all it's worth, although I have a feeling that all his flannel is for nothing, because today's the day. I just know it. Today's the day when Herb'e parts with his most treasured possession – his secret.

Dan lowers the microphone and waits as the photographers in the audience navigate through rows of people and down the long steps leading to the pool. I have just rounded off the dolphins' last trick with a feed and a long blast on the whistle, and the audience has responded enthusiastically. It's a great feeling.

Today, we have a good house – especially for the time of year – nearly six hundred people, maybe more. The whole building echoes with excited chatter, and the crowd's delight at being so close to real, live dolphins is reflected in bright smiles and eyes that follow Duchess and Herb'e everywhere they go.

Herb'e? Well, that's Flippa's real name. Flippa is only a stage name, adopted to satisfy the expectations of the public, who visit a dolphin show *wanting* to see a *Flippa*, just like in the movies. And what the public want, they get.

The sun streams through the skylights, reflecting off blue water. Today my *enchanted mirror* is sparking electricity. Duchess is already mentally preparing; I feel the tension building in her. This is Duchess' big moment, her cameo performance. I indicate to Herb'e to move out of the way and, as usual at this point, he meanders off to a corner of the pool, where, hopefully, he'll dilly-dally around until the trick is finished.

Dilly-dally around? Who am I kidding? The radio's on. I can hear the static echoing in my ears. He has invoked a silent *connection*. I can literally feel his nervous excitement as he scurries around inside my head, preparing me mentally, fine-tuning me, so that when it happens, I'll have crystal clear reception.

"I know your game, Herb'e. You've got me hooked, and you're slowly reeling me in."

The frequency is wide open, but he's still not saying anything. He doesn't want to spoil the moment.

Cameras jostle for position over the safety barriers, then become still. The hum of conversation ceases. There is silence.

Duchess is bobbing in the water just before me, watching me intently. I take a breath, signal for her to momentarily hold her position, then throw out my right arm.

"Go!"

She dives.

To execute this trick, Duchess needs to pick up considerable speed. She usually does two laps of the pool, circling faster and faster, building momentum, tension, energy, then on the third lap she shoots out of the water missile-fashion, climbing higher, higher, higher, until she can reach the ball and bash it with her 'nose'. This done, she free falls into the water, showering everyone in the first two rows of the dolphinarium.

Now, every living thing in the place holds its breath – even Herb'e, as he watches assiduously from his corner. The atmosphere is charged. Just beneath the water's surface, Duchess speeds… lap one… building nicely… lap two… almost ready…

Suddenly, Herb'e shoots across Duchess' path! At these speeds, a collision could be catastrophic, and Duchess has to swerve to avoid him, twisting her body awkwardly. She thrusts her head out of the water, glares at him, then dashes towards me, bobbing her head frenziedly and literally screaming with rage.

"Look what he's done to my trick! Look what he's done!"

I stare helplessly. I know what's coming. He's spoiled Duchess' trick deliberately so that he can outdo her. There has always been rivalry between the dolphins, but this intentional act of sabotage has been a long time in the planning. I glance at Dan, who is also staring goggle-eyed at the dolphins, microphone drooping in his hand.

Then, unbelievably, Herb'e takes up lapping the pool, just as Duchess had been doing moments earlier, a dark figure just beneath the water's surface, travelling faster and faster… building speed, momentum, energy… lap one… lap two…

Dan and I continue to watch breathlessly. The audience watches, silent and confused. Only Duchess doesn't watch, her eyes fixed firmly on me as she continues to remonstrate.

But I see only Herb'e. I have an inkling… a faint hope… it's coming… it's going to happen.

Herb'e arcs out of the water, rising higher, higher, higher… and suddenly everything goes into slow motion. He starts to spin and, as I watch, I will his body around, lifting him, turning him, mentally spinning him through the air.

"That's it, Herb'e, go for it!"

I'd been working on this trick for months, but getting nowhere. So exhausted, so frustrated and disappointed had I been at our failure, I'd actually given up. And now Herb'e's doing it: he's doing the trick I've always dreamed about, the trick that will put my dolphins – and me – at the top of our field in Europe.

As he completes a full one and a half forward somersault, splashing back into the pool and drenching me with water, I stand frozen. The trick replays in my mind, still in slow-mo, whilst the realisation of what he's just done fully sinks in.

Herb'e has given me – and the audience – a trick never before seen in Britain! I can't even be sure that it's been seen in Europe. He has somersaulted through the air and seized the crown for us all.

It's also startlingly clear that he knows what he's done, and has planned it to make the biggest impact: first, ruin Duchess' starring moment; second, blow everyone away with something even bigger… even better. I'd thought he just didn't understand. Now, I know that he's been prevaricating – and extorting fish out of me for months and months and months!

Irrelevant now. My chest is thudding, and my mind feels like it's reeling through a wormhole. I start to blow the whistle, one blast for every piece of fish.

Herb'e resurfaces and shoots towards me, his gleeful dolphin voice echoing as I bombard him with fish and loud excited whistles.

Whistle – fish! Whistle – fish! Whistle – fish!

Suddenly, I think, Signal, signal… what you doing, Capello? You need a signal! Think! And the Roman salute leaps into my mind. I tightly curl the fingers of my right hand, then throw my arm across my chest, rapping my shoulder with my fist. Once, twice, three times.

Whistle – fish! Salute! Whistle – fish! Salute!

Two whistles – two fish! Salute! Two whistles – two fish! Salute!

Three whistles – three fish! Salute!

Herb'e catches his reward deftly, laughing noisily at his own cleverness and the treasury of food raining down upon him.

Duchess screams even louder. *"What are you doing? What are you doing?"*

She's confused. All she can hear is the whistle blowing and Herb'e's triumphant cries as fish pour into his open mouth.

"Why are you feeding him? Why are you feeding him? He ruined my trick!"

As my left hand showers Herb'e with fish, my right hand reaches sympathetically for Duchess.

"I know, girl, I know. I'll tell you in a minute."

I don't speak verbally, but with my mind, because that's the way you speak to dolphins, the way you *really* speak. The *connection* – the one I talk about, the one the managers scoff at – is white-hot now.

It's always there, the *connection*, even during the calmest times: the conversation between me and my dolphins that happens only in our minds. The only downside is that it always leaves me drained. I can't count how many times I've staggered off stage, exhausted by it. But this time, it's different: my mind is racing, my body numb to everything except the tingling of my nerves. I'm on a rush, higher than I've ever been. But I am not alone. There are three of us on this ride: Duchess, Herb'e, me. Three minds, three conversations: a conference where everyone's shouting at once. It's chaos, but the sort of chaos that kick-started the universe, chaos with intention, chaos with order.

"You've got to show Duch, Herb'e."

"But HE RUINED MY TRICK!"

"I know, Duch… I know… I'll tell you…"

And Herb'e's laughter.

All doors are slung open. We're in the loop. His glee, her anger, my excitement.

I drop to my knees, extending arms and pulling them both into an embrace, holding them: comforting her, congratulating him, relishing the feel of their warm, wet faces against mine.

Then, somewhere a million miles away, I hear the bewildered murmurings of the audience. The audience! I'd completely forgotten about them. Glancing up, I take in the bemused expressions, the shaking heads. They haven't a clue what's happening. They waited for a highball. They didn't get it; and now they aren't going to get it. And what's more, I don't care. I couldn't give a damn, because I've got something better… *we've* got something better!

Dan is watching us, Duchess, Herb'e and me, arms hanging loosely by his side, confusion in his eyes. He doesn't know what's happening either, and though he should be calming the crowd, covering for the turmoil, he just doesn't know what to say.

I struggle for breath, my voice little more than a gasp. "Tell them that they've just seen a full one and a half forward somersault, never before known in the UK, nor probably in the whole of Europe."

Dan lifts the microphone to his mouth, his words reverberating throughout the dolphinarium, a meaningless confusion of noise inside my head.

My mind is already back with Duchess and Herb'e.

The crowd ceases to exist.

The compère ceases to exist.

The show is ruined, but that doesn't matter.

Everything is in shadow; but we three are cocooned in a light, blinding in its brilliance.

Dolphin heads nodding, shaking…

Dolphin voices shouting, celebrating…

We're on a rollercoaster, flying away on Herb'e's laughter… flying so fast that I can almost feel the drag as we whizz back in time to where it all began…

❧ 1 ❧

"The cocky sod!" My irate partner slams a fish bucket onto the draining board, sparking lightning bolts across the kitchen. "Who does he think he is, waltzing in here and talking to you like that? Acts like he owns the bloody place…"

"Who are you talking about, Vance?" I reply, studiously thumbing the pages of Herb'e's logbook.

"You know damn well who… HIM! That big-shot transporter… the one who thinks he knows it all."

I can understand how Vance is feeling, because the transporter seriously ticked me off too. "Don't let him get to you, Vance. He's not worth it – just another bum with delusions of grandeur."

"Well, I don't like his attitude and I'll be glad when he's pissed off back to wherever he came from!"

Crash, bang, wallop…! Jesus, Vance is certainly giving them fish buckets some stick!

"Another thing, did you *clock* how pally he was with Tommy? For a minute there, I thought he was gonna snog him!"

Urghhh… the very thought gives me the creeps. "Yeah, they *were* a bit friendly – reminded me of long-lost brothers."

Vance's shadow falls across the table. "Long-lost *cronies*, more like!"

"Bloody hell, Vance, you're like a dog with a bone. For God's sake, give it a rest, because you're doing my head in. Look, why don't you go help Beryl muck out Smelly and Worse, then clean the fish buckets later? That way, you can keep an eye on Tommy's blast from the past and I can get on with writing the morning logs in peace."

"Oh, trying to get rid of me, are you? Charmin', that is!"

Trying to get rid of him? Where did he get that idea? "Come on, Vance, gimme me a break..."

"Okay, I'm going, I'm going! I know when I'm not wanted."

A slamming door finds me finally sitting alone. Peace, blessed peace. At last, I can concentrate on the job in hand.

Now, what do I write in these rotten logbooks? I could start with 'the wheel's about to fall off', but that might sound a bit too dramatic. So I have to think this through... be creative...

The blank page blurs before my eyes – a black hole slowly sucking me in.

God, this is ridiculous... absolutely crazy. Instead of sitting here worrying about what to write, I should be complaining at the highest level. But that would mean going over Tommy's head – hardly conducive to good staff relations. Besides, even if I did make this official, the men in suits wouldn't listen; they'd just rally around their new golden boy.

So, for now, all I can do is write up my log entry and try to convey my feeling of desperation. But how? How do I put that into words?

I suppose I could repeat my original warning that bringing two extra dolphins to Hendle will cause serious overcrowding...

... point out how it will place even more pressure on our rotten, lousy filtration system...

... a system that can't cope with four dolphins, let alone six...

... a fact that will only become apparent when we find ourselves having to dump bad water on a daily basis...

... something my esteemed colleague and general manager, Tommy Backhouse, won't allow under any circumstances, because that would mean breaking precious Company policy...

... a policy which unequivocally states that we cannot ditch water unless it's deemed a health hazard...

... and only then after full consultation between vets and Management...

… in other words, yet another convenient excuse for Head Office not to spend money.

"That's it… jobs a good 'un… penguins sorted!" The door crashes open. "Only the fish buckets to do now…"

I throw Vance another beseeching look and he stops short.

"What? Don't tell me you haven't written those logs yet? I mean, how hard can it be?"

Is he trying to wind me up or what? Biting my lip, I point to the door.

"All right, all right… you don't have to say anything… I get the message…I'm going, I'm going…"

I wince as the door slams behind him. Silence. Alone again, thank God.

Now, where was I? Thoughtfully rolling my pen between my fingers, I realise that I really need to talk this through with someone – preferably someone *not* emotionally involved. So, who's going to listen to me? Who?

The reply materialises in the vision of a friendly face.

Gerry… yes, Gerry, that's who… Gerry Mansell at West Coast. He'll listen. I'll give him a call and…

A sudden feeling of deflation washes over me as my reverie is cut short. No, not Gerry, definitely not Gerry, because he's got enough on his plate as it is, especially since the arrival of King Tommy.

Gerry might be head trainer, but he's definitely fallen out of favour with the men in suits – certainly a strange turn of events, as there was a time when the Company felt he could do no wrong. Yet another solemn reminder of just how fickle this business is.

The click of a handle as the kitchen door opens yet again.

"Oh no, Vance, please… please… what do you want now?"

"It's that new dolphin, Clyde… I've been watching him." Vance's voice is thick with concern. "He's hanging around Duchess and Herb'e's pen with his nose stuck through the bars issuing challenges."

Poor Vance – he thinks he's telling me something I don't already know. "Yeah, he started threatening Herb'e the minute we put him into the water. And what's more, this is just the beginning."

Vance stiffens. "What do you mean, 'just the beginning'?"

Exasperated, I can't help snapping. "What do you want me to do, Vance, draw you a picture? Clyde's on a campaign of intimidation. In other words, he's picking a fight."

The colour visibly drains from Vance's face. "Picking a fight? But Herb'e won't stand a chance against Clyde... he's only a baby!"

Vance is right: Herb'e *is* only a baby and has no chance against a fully mature male like Clyde. Like it or not, my poor Herb'e is about to learn first-hand the darker side of dolphin culture. Even worse, even more galling, I'll be powerless to stop it.

And with that bleak realisation, everything becomes clear. Returning my gaze to the blank page of Herb'e's logbook, I pick up my pen and begin to write:

15th January 1973, Black Monday... the arrival of Bonnie and Clyde.

Back at the flat, Vance and I set to work formulating a plan to limit the disruption caused by our two new houseguests, which wasn't going to be easy.

Both Bonnie and Clyde were two fully mature dolphins who had been in captivity for a staggering thirteen years. This had earned them the title of 'oldest working dolphins in Europe' – extraordinary in itself, as the lifespan of a show dolphin was estimated at little more than four years at best. A far cry from the thirty years' life expectancy in the wild.

Bonnie and Clyde's unprecedented time around their many human gaolers would have taught them virtually everything there was to know about human behaviour, so I was under no illusions about the mammoth task facing me – especially with Clyde. This canny dolphin had a fierce reputation, allegedly surviving on a staple diet of trainers and presenters. Controlling him would be difficult, if not impossible.

Even so, there was no denying that the two halves of this famous duo were visually impressive – Bonnie in particular. Physically, she was imposing – a perfect dolphin specimen, incredibly powerfully built and sporting a bull neck and beautiful silver-grey colouring. Her graceful eight-foot form was sleek and chiselled, and put me in mind of a living torpedo. She was literally magnificent.

Clyde, however, was totally different. Physically, he was nowhere near as compact, his body being long, almost stringy in comparison. But his colour was remarkable. Even after thirteen years of chlorine bleaching, his skin pigmentation was still a striking slate grey, meaning that he must have been virtually black in the wild – a true rarity in a bottlenose dolphin.

"So what are we going to do about Bonnie and Clyde?" Vance muttered for the hundredth time. "And what's going to happen with Duchess and Herb'e? I mean, what are we gonna do? Come on, talk to me! You've hardly said a word since we got home."

He was obviously still very upset at the thought of Herb'e being menaced – and he wasn't the only one. *I* was still finding it difficult to shake the vision of a motionless Clyde blanketing the entrance to Duchess and Herb'e's pen.

"Tell you the truth, Vance, I'm not sure what to do. It stands to reason that we can't keep Duchess and Herb'e penned forever. Eventually, we've got to let them out, and we don't need a crystal ball to tell us what's gonna happen next."

A concerned grunt, then Vance reached for his cigarettes. "What about Baby and Scouse? Do you think they'll be all right?"

I clocked the smoke funnels welling from his nostrils. "They should be okay for the time being. Up to press, the only thing on Clyde's mind is Herb'e. But once he's sorted him out, everyone will be fair game."

The smoke rings generated by Vance's cigarette slow-danced through the air, hypnotically weaving a delicate journey to the ceiling. As I gradually became transfixed by his nicotine-fuelled fairies, my workmate's voice began to fade into dreamland and I again found myself drifting into that wistful, sweet-smelling nausea... along with the strangest sensation that I'd never actually left the dolphinarium.

But, even more disturbing, was an accompanying feeling of overwhelming panic and fear...

Then, it hit me! I was experiencing a psychic call: a *connection* was kicking in.

Yet how was that possible? The dolphinarium was literally miles away.

❦ 3 ❧

That familiar light-headedness and the obligatory headache further confirmed what I already knew. Someone was tapping into my mind, trying to open a *connection*. However, this psychic bonding was strangely different from any I had experienced before. Moreover, whoever had initiated the link was obviously having trouble getting through, almost as if they were operating from a distance.

Could this really be happening?

Closing my eyes, I strived to look deeper. Suddenly, there was the face of my mystery caller – one I instantly recognised – Herb'e.

In his panic, my terrified dolphin had beamed me a long-range SOS and, unbelievably, I'd picked it up. Even more incredible, our link was being strengthened by a shared vision – a waking dream – something I'd never experienced before. It was as if I were actually seeing through Herb'e's eyes, experiencing Herb'e's fear.

Through the bars of Duchess and Herb'e's holding pen, I could clearly see the shadowy figure of Clyde looking in...

... and, even worse, I sensed that this sinister dolphin knew it.

With a shudder of horror, I realised that Clyde had somehow managed to invade my shared *connection* with Herb'e, purposely tapping into our signal to eavesdrop. The psychic bond was no longer shared by two: it was shared by three. Clyde's darkness was now fully in the mix.

My shock at discovering that our link had been compromised immediately initiated its breakdown, allowing the few indistinct sights and sounds remaining to be gobbled up by a hungry static. Holding my breath, I strained to reconnect, but the radio had been unplugged. Herb'e had gone.

"Hey, buggerlugs, are you listening to me or have you nodded off?" A familiar voice broke my dream.

"No, Vance, no… just thinking…"

Vance revved one final drag out of his cigarette, then fumbled for the ashtray. "Do you want a brew? I could murder a cup of char."

Difficult to speak as my mind was still out of sync, so I just gave him a grateful nod.

Everything seemed a little hazy – everything, that is, except for the haunting vision of Clyde's dark shape drifting ominously outside the entrance to Duchess and Herb'e's holding pen.

❧ 4 ❧

By the end of the night, Vance and I had reluctantly agreed that penning our two dolphin teams could only ever be a short-term solution. Eventually, we'd have to give them the freedom of the pool, effectively leaving them at the mercy of Clyde. Distressing as this might be, we had no other option but to allow nature to take its course.

We'd also decided on extending the nightly backwashes whilst continuing to keep Tommy blissfully unaware of our hidden agenda of water dumping. However, even then, if we were to stand any chance of maintaining water quality, we'd have to administer more chlorine.

One thing in our favour: the off-season park was almost deserted, meaning we wouldn't be faced with the added complication of giving shows – although this was a luxury soon to be cut short. In fact, the very next morning, Tommy called me into his office to deliver some bad news.

"I've received a new directive from Head Office," he told me. "We're in the winter season now, so every penny counts, which means that, from now on, no audience will be deemed too small to command a show. And, since Bonnie and Clyde are already in the main pool, it seems sensible to let them do the performances."

Was it my imagination, or had Tommy's demeanour changed? Suddenly, he seemed uncharacteristically officious, that easy manner gone. He was no longer asking, but telling.

Of course, as if to prove a point, by mid-morning we had twelve lost souls sitting expectantly in the auditorium, meaning, whether we liked it or not, the show was on.

Vance compèred whilst I presented – a strange experience for me, because I'd never before worked dolphins that I hadn't trained myself. However, Bonnie and Clyde's trick list was virtually identical to Duchess and Herb'e's, missing only the back somersault. But, they *did* perform a double beaching trick, where they leapt onto the stage to lie motionless together with their tails held high in the air – a spectacular trick that I'd long admired, and truly incredible to see.

Bonnie and Clyde were without doubt ultra-professional, performing with supreme confidence. Bonnie had a beautiful temperament and a willing disposition. Clyde, on the other hand, was the complete opposite, bullying Bonnie and doing his best to derail the show. I quickly became aware that, for him, this first performance was more about testing the water and probing for weaknesses than wanting to please. Even at this early stage, he was giving me fair warning of his intent: Clyde is top dog, number one… so get used to it!

His behaviour confirmed my theory that this highly intelligent and crafty dolphin had little respect for humankind. He was clearly used to getting his own way, meaning that mental blackmail would be of little use against him. He showed scant interest in performing, waltzing through the show in a nonchalant, disruptive manner. In fact, his only interest seemed to be in threatening Herb'e between tricks – a disquieting indicator of things to come.

Even so, by the end of the show, I had begrudgingly conceded that Bonnie and Clyde were a very impressive team. Their professionalism had shone through, despite Clyde's antics, and it wasn't hard to see why they were so highly prized. Still, in fairness, they'd had a lot of practice – thirteen years, to be precise – whilst my babies were still only learning.

After the performance, an elated Tommy floated down from his office. "These are the best dolphins in the country," he enthused, "simply the best!"

I immediately struck back. "They're good – but the best are stuck in a holding pen less than fifteen feet away."

Bonnie and Clyde might be top *individual* performers, but the dream *team* was unmistakably Duchess and Herb'e.

As the working day ended, I reluctantly released all my dolphins to join Bonnie and Clyde in the main pool – although just how I'd get them back in their pens tomorrow was anyone's guess.

Immediately, Clyde resumed his intimidation of Herb'e, knowing that the fight he so longed for was now near at hand. And, even during our customary swim, his relentless intimidation forced a frightened Herb'e into shadowing either Duchess or me.

"Stay away from Herb'e, Clyde… just stay away! I'm watching you."

A threat which, of course, Clyde blatantly ignored.

Silently snaking through the water, he continued his terror tactics… Clyde was on a mission.

❧ 5 ❧

That night, I had a guilt-ridden sleep, worrying about Herb'e, painting worst-case scenarios and feeling that I'd somehow deserted him in his hour of need. "Come on, Vance, rise and shine," I shouted, as he tried to dig his way back under his blankets.

"What time is it?" he mumbled.

"Doesn't matter – get up, I'm worried about Herb'e."

"Go away!"

I practically wrestled him out of his bed and, minutes later, we were speeding to the dolphinarium. "God, I hope he's all right."

Dashing from the car, I feverishly unlocked the door and entered the pool, almost too frightened to look. To my relief, all was quiet, the six dolphins schooling in semi-slumber, bodies softly weaving the water.

"Thank goodness, Herb'e seems okay," I whispered. But then I looked closer: across his back were the ragged lacerations of razor sharp dolphin teeth. "Oh no! Vance, look at the state of his back... he's slashed to pieces! That rotten bastard's really done a number on him!"

Vance's face creased with concern. "That's not all, he's had a go at Duchess, too – look at her forehead."

Three angry scars ran like tramlines across her melon.

"Oh no... my beautiful dolphins..." I bellowed. "In less than twelve hours, that vicious sod has scarred them for life! I'll kill him!"

"Well, now we know who's top dog, don't we?" Vance groaned, scanning the pool. "But at least Baby and Scouse look okay."

My God... Baby and Scouse! I'd been so preoccupied with Duchess

18

and Herb'e that I'd completely forgotten about them. My tiny duo wouldn't stand a chance against the might of Clyde, especially with their handicaps. Baby, in particular, would prove a tempting morsel for him, being just an infant with no knowledge of the unpalatable side of dolphin society. And poor Scouse wouldn't fare much better, having lost both his eyes during that botched transport from the States.

"Yeah, they're okay for now," I replied darkly, "but, believe me, it won't take Clyde long to remedy that."

Baby and Scouse had been spared Clyde's attentions this time because they didn't yet represent a threat. But it would only be a matter of time before they too tasted his wrath. This, unfortunately, was the way of dolphin culture.

I recalled my chat with the young American transporter, when he had described how the catchers chose their dolphins. Dolphin society was split into two camps. The first consisted mainly of young virile males who would spend virtually all their time sparring and indulging in violent sex play. Practically all its members were badly marked, rendering them undesirable to dolphinariums.

The second consisted of the young, the old and the vulnerable, guided and protected by fully mature carers. This school was normally led by a big mama dolphin – very similar to Bonnie – strong and powerful, yet caring.

Every so often, the two schools collided, allowing all the strong, randy males to indulge in a chaotic dolphin gangbang with the young females of breeding age. Then, job done, they'd be on their way, leaving the young females pregnant, and the weaker males to swell the ranks of the mixed school.

Many members of this mixed school were young, clean and unmarked, and it was these who were in demand. Pretty dolphins brought a high price on the open market, begging the question, how did we end up with poor Scouse?

Because, much as I cared for him, Scouse was no doubt the proverbial ugly duckling.

{❧ 6 ❧}

Despite my anger over Duchess and Herb'e's injuries, I remained patently aware that at some point during the morning, I would have to embark on the daunting task of getting four unco-operative dolphins back into the holding pens.

I'd already decided that I wanted to gate Bonnie and Clyde rather than Duchess and Herb'e, but just how to achieve it was a problem. The gangster pairing would not surrender the freedom of the main pool gladly and, with the large number of dolphins involved, my gating system was now redundant. I had no choice but to use what I loathed most: the net.

Fortunately, just like North Liston, the Hendle pool had attracted many helpers, all eager to share in the dolphin experience. Most were students from the local university, working to supplement their grants. So, whenever short of manpower, I would routinely call on them.

Reaching for the telephone, I began summoning my volunteers.

Throughout the morning, my helpers drifted in one by one. Even our general manager, Tommy, left the sanctity of his office to lend a hand.

As always, the first to arrive were Carol and Graham – my two most trusted and loyal volunteers. Graham was just sixteen years old and simply loved being around dolphins. Carol's interest, however, was altogether more serious. A striking eighteen-year-old brunette studying marine biology at the local uni, she came across as a typical women's libber – curt and lippy. She often gave me the impression that she thought me chauvinistic, and tolerated rather than liked me – which was a shame, as I found her very attractive. Just a pity the feeling wasn't mutual. But, at the end of the day, if she wanted to study dolphins, there literally wasn't anywhere else for her to go – mine was the only show in town.

Once all my volunteers were in place, we opened the left hand pen. To everyone's surprise, Baby and Scouse immediately swam inside, no doubt eager to get away from the clutches of Clyde.

It was the same story with the right hand pen: the gate had barely swung open before Duchess and Herb'e barged their way in, also keen to escape Clyde's attentions.

"Oh no," I gasped, "this isn't what I wanted." Four dolphins gated and not a net in sight. Normally, a great result. Only problem: wrong dolphins.

"You may as well leave Bonnie and Clyde in the main pool," Tommy suggested. "It'll save a lot of trouble."

"No, I want to get them out while I have enough people to manage the net." I turned to Duchess and Herb'e.

"Right, you two, you're not hiding in that pen all day. I want you back in the main pool."

But they had no intentions of leaving, and it took some prodding and pushing with the hurdle-pole to usher them out.

"My God, Vance, I've never known them like this. They're absolutely terrified." I glanced darkly at Clyde. "Now, let's get *him* out of the way."

But as we lowered the net into the water, total chaos erupted. All the dolphins began darting about, making it impossible to separate the two panicking teams. Crafty Clyde, guessing our intention, repeatedly thwarted us by purposely shadowing either Duchess or Herb'e. It took well over an hour before we eventually succeeded in forcing him and Bonnie into the pen.

"Thank God," I sighed. "Now I can start working Duchess and Herb'e in peace. Thanks everyone… superb job. What would I do without you?"

Unfortunately, by the time all my volunteers had departed, we already had an audience of fourteen punters sitting in the auditorium, leaving us no time for a much-needed break – not even a quick brew. It was straight into another performance.

The show started out well, despite the squawks of anger emanating from Clyde, who was clearly disgruntled at being caged. Nevertheless, it was blatantly obvious that his unceasing din was unsettling Duchess and Herb'e, as both dolphins, eyes bright with anxiety, repeatedly glanced towards his pen.

"Come on, you two, ignore him. Concentrate on the performance."

But, as time went on, Clyde took his frustration to a physical level, violently throwing his weight against the gate to rattle it loudly. This bodily assault continued relentlessly, distracting both performers and audience alike.

Meanwhile, Duchess and Herb'e were growing ever more jumpy. Did they know something I didn't?

Kneeling, I cupped their heads and tried to reassure them.

"Come on. Try not to worry about him – he can't do anything from there."
However, I spoke too soon...

To my horror, Clyde suddenly launched himself over the gate of the pen and propelled himself at a terrifying speed towards an unsuspecting Herb'e.

"My God, he's out!" I screamed.

Panic engulfed the entire auditorium as the black torpedo literally tore the mirror apart. Clyde powered through the water, zeroing in on Herb'e with a ruthless precision to ram his entire body clear of its surface. A winded Herb'e fell back into the pool with a sickening thud, body limp and half-floating. And, with Herb'e now helpless, the malevolent Clyde wasted no time in following up his sneak attack with a relentless beating.

The small audience recoiled in horror and disbelief. This wasn't what they'd come to see... this wasn't what they'd expected...

Vance gasped, face draining of colour. "My God, what are we gonna do? What are we gonna do?"

"I know what *I'm* gonna do," I growled, snatching at the hurdle-pole. "I'm gonna give him a taste of his own medicine."

"You can't, David, you can't..." Vance hissed, grabbing my arm. "Audience present... Don't forget the audience...!"

Vance was right. With an audience looking on, I could do nothing but stand helplessly by, listening to Herb'e's screams. Tormented beyond belief, I gritted my teeth and glared up at Tommy, who watched from the shadows at the back of the auditorium. This is your fault, I thought bitterly. But for you, this psycho dolphin wouldn't even be here!

Some three torturous minutes passed before a smug and triumphant Clyde finally permitted my battered Herb'e to flee to the corner of the pool. Then, unbelievably, Clyde had the nerve to take Herb'e's place by Duchess' side.

Vance looked at me bewilderedly. "What do we do? Carry on?"

I again glared up at Tommy. "No – show's over."

"What about the public?"

"I don't care about the rotten public!"

However, the cocky Clyde disagreed. Fixing me with a stare, he remained bobbing at my feet, waiting for the performance to continue.

And it was then that I experienced his cold, dark *connection* for the first time.

"What are you waiting for? Carry on with the show. I'm here now."

I stood on the poolside, rigid with rage.

"Not a chance in hell, Clyde, you rotten, lousy bastard!"

In the distance, I could hear Vance apologising to the audience for the show's premature end. Meanwhile, Clyde never moved, but remained at the foot of the stage, leering up at me. As I held his arrogant stare, I found it increasingly hard to maintain my self-control.

Whilst a disappointed and bemused audience trickled through the exit doors, a stony-faced Tommy descended the auditorium steps, clearly annoyed that we'd ended the show when we could have continued with Clyde. But I didn't care. Disappointed audience or not, I had no intention of allowing Clyde to rob Herb'e of his place. Body rigid, I continued to glare down at him.

Unrelenting, the belligerent dolphin held his ground, fixing me with his insolent gaze, smiling mouth twisted into a challenging smirk. *"Nothing you can do."*

Clyde was evidently taking enormous pleasure in goading me. *"Nothing…"*

I could hardly bear to look at him…

"Not a single thing…"

Fury, uncontrollable fury…

As the dolphinarium door banged shut, the pressure valve within exploded.

"No audience now, you bastard! No audience now…"

I took a standing leap at him from the stage. But, in my frenzied rage, I'd forgotten that the *connection* works both ways and by the time I'd hit the water… he'd gone.

Fully clothed and wearing heavy wellies, I plummeted to the pool floor, from where I was forced to grapple my way back up the pool wall and onto the stage. As I dragged myself from the water, my wet clothes emanated steam. "If I get my hands on him, I'll kill him! I swear it, I'll kill him!"

And didn't Clyde know it? Drifting a safe *jumping* distance away, he observed me through narrowed eyes.

Tommy approached, smiling tensely. "Calm down, David, calm down. Are you okay?"

"No, I'm not bloody okay!" I growled. "I need to keep that vicious bastard away from my dolphins. I need a boom and I need one fast!"

Several hours passed before I regained sufficient composure to hold a logical conversation. "Look, Tommy, Clyde will pull this stunt again and again – no doubt about it. He has to be stopped and stopped now or he'll cause chaos… absolute chaos. I need a boom – one that extends at least three feet above the waterline so that *that thing* can't jump over it."

Tommy agreed without hesitation. "Yes, you're right, we can't allow Clyde to jeopardize the shows… I'll get onto it straight away." The horrific thought of show cancellations had prompted the answer I needed.

Nonetheless, this gave me little comfort. Today, the storm clouds had officially rolled in and the chaos I'd predicted had begun. The Hendle pool was now in the grip of a bombastic and vengeful Clyde, and I felt powerless to stop him. I was also acutely aware that in just one day this dolphin's antics had very nearly driven me into overstepping the line – a further reminder of my dependence on medication.

Sadly, it didn't look like I'd be coming off the Valium any time soon.

⟨ 8 ⟩

We decided to site the boom on the left-hand side of the pool, effectively cutting a large chunk off its oval shape. It wouldn't be pretty – in fact, it would look like something off a building site – but there was no other solution. Clyde had to be checked. However, the boom would take another fifteen days to complete, meaning we still had at least another fortnight of hell to endure.

But Clyde wasn't the only problem: even with high quantities of chlorine and constant backwashing, the water was again deteriorating at an alarming rate. We urgently needed a partial pool dump – something obvious to everyone except Tommy, who refused authorisation, as usual. So now, not only did I have the worry of a psychotic Clyde tearing up my dolphins, but I also had the unenviable task of watching them slowly burning in their own waste.

During this period of mayhem, Gerry telephoned – a rare occurrence since Tommy's arrival. It seemed that he too was having water problems at West Coast, although Management there had at least agreed to a partial dump.

"It's all down to these bloody archaic filtration systems," he told me.

"Archaic? What do you mean, archaic? These pools are brand new."

"The pools might be brand new, but the filtration equipment isn't," he replied. "The Company bought them in second-hand from disused swimming pools to save money."

I couldn't believe what I was hearing. "Second-hand? You've got to be joking. No wonder the filters can't cope – they were never meant to deal with dolphins in the first place. What was the Company thinking of?"

"Money… what else? That's all the men in suits ever care about." Gerry's voice suddenly dropped. "I know it's hard, Dave, but you've got to try to lighten up. Remember, dolphinariums don't just break dolphins, they break people, too."

Something I wasn't likely to forget. It was common knowledge that almost all the best trainers suffered from deep psychological problems – a road I was already heading down.

Reading into my silence, Gerry decided to wind up his call. But not before delivering a chilling message: "Dave, I'm warning you: watch out for Backhouse. I know this guy from old. I know his form and, I'm telling you, one day he'll knife you in the back."

I made no comment, but replaced the receiver thoughtfully. So my suspicions were correct: Tommy and Gerry had indeed clashed in the past.

It was true that, since Tommy's arrival, Gerry's nose had been well and truly pushed out, begging the question, was Gerry's remark merely vindictive, or did Tommy indeed hide a darker side? Only time would tell.

However, I was painfully aware that their feud might one day put me in a difficult position. Gerry was Company head trainer and my friend. But Tommy was general manager and someone I had to work with on a daily basis. If I wasn't careful, I could easily end up being the meat in the sandwich.

On a brighter note, armed with my newly acquired knowledge about the origins of the filtration equipment, I should hopefully be able to convince Tommy to authorise at least a partial ditch.

Then again, judging by his past form, I wouldn't hold my breath.

❦ 9 ❧

Circumstances being what they were, it had become impossible to remove Bonnie and Clyde from the main pool, which meant that they got to perform all the shows whilst my dolphins remained incarcerated in their pens.

Vance and I took turns presenting and compèring and, thanks to Clyde's antics, I was fast developing a line in glib patter. The gangster dolphin was a nightmare, disrupting performances at every opportunity. In fact, if it hadn't been for Bonnie's good-natured reliability, the shows might well have collapsed.

However, Bonnie's compliance didn't fit with Clyde's plans, so, in an attempt to stop her working, he embarked on a vicious campaign of snout butting – but only during shows. He was crafty enough to know that I couldn't discipline him with an audience present. All I could do was intervene by forcibly pushing him away from Bonnie. Yet, for Clyde, even this feeble act was unacceptable, triggering frenzied tantrums, which always ended with him leaving the stage and refusing to work.

Clyde took great pleasure in holding me to ransom and, somehow, I had to fight back. With nothing else to lose, I decided to reintroduce the mind games – the good girl/bad boy tactics that had been so successful with Duchess and Herb'e in the past. So, each time Clyde battered Bonnie, I fed *her*, but not him, in the hope of teaching him that bullying didn't pay.

I continued this ploy for a full week, but it only served to make matters worse. This clever dolphin had been scanning trainers and presenters for well over thirteen years, so knew all the tricks. For him, my futile game held no surprises.

But the *real* issue for Clyde was *me*. He'd realised that I was very different from his normal human adversaries. My ability to access the complex workings of the dolphin radio had got him rattled, which was something this domineering and controlling dolphin wasn't used to. He couldn't figure out just how I'd managed to acquire my special psychic gift. All he knew was that it made me very dangerous. Clyde now viewed me, not just as a mystery, but a threat.

His domination of the Hendle dolphins had been achieved swiftly and effortlessly.

He was now working on a new agenda…

… domination of me.

⟨ 10 ⟩

My special psychic gift…

… the gangster Clyde would never know of that first, breath-taking encounter, that life-changing experience. Never know how the king he hoped to usurp had found his very reason for reigning within the dark confines of a transport van: Duchess… my beautiful, beautiful Duchess.

I vividly recalled how her radiance had pierced the gloom, drawing me to her like a moth to a flame – a magical baptism, creating a bond that would link us forever.

Moreover, our coming together had taught me to question my once-rigid interpretation of the world around me, because, in the dolphin realm, things were never what they seemed – never just black and white. The dolphin mind held many rooms, a few of which I was free to enter – a privilege that, in Clyde's eyes, elevated my status from that of human to dolphin. To him, I was the alpha male – the only remaining barrier to pool domination. This was no longer about putting me in my place. This was now all-out war.

But I had been forearmed.

Duchess and Herb'e had taught me that the *connection* could take many forms, the most sinister being the *silent link*. This I compared to a telephone call, where the caller hung on the line, refusing to speak – eerie and intimidating.

Clyde had evoked this kind of *connection* on several occasions, creating for himself a room within a room, from where he could scan me without fear of reciprocation. Once within the confines of this retreat, he was impossible to engage – untouchable – meaning I had to look elsewhere to find his Achilles' Heel.

It was imperative that Clyde be disciplined – something I wasn't capable of doing myself. So I desperately needed an ally – someone to do it for me... someone at least equal in stature to Clyde himself.

Bonnie... all roads led to Bonnie. Maybe she was the answer. After all, she wasn't a young, emotional female like Duchess. She was a powerhouse mama dolphin, capable of leading a mixed school in the wild. If I could encourage her to stand up for herself and go head-to-head with Clyde, she could well be *his* undoing... and *my* saviour. All she needed was a push in the right direction. And I had plenty of 'push' to offer.

As the days progressed, Clyde became ever more desperate in his quest to prevent Bonnie performing. Upping the ante, he intensified his aggression by battering her ever more viciously about the face whenever she came into the stage. It was as if he were ramming home the point that she should answer to only one ruler – him.

Day by day, hour by hour, I watched as Bonnie's pleasant disposition began to ebb away, watched as Clyde's constant beatings took their toll on this gentle giant. Bonnie was reaching the end of her tether – I could see it in her eyes.

Unbeknown to Clyde, he had unwittingly given me the green light. Now was the time to act. Now was the time to give Bonnie a little encouragement.

"You can't allow him to keep doing this, Bonnie. You've got to fight back."

Although I could feel her anguish, I could also sense her growing rage. Deep inside, a volcano was rumbling.

As usual, after the early show had finished, I spent some time with Bonnie, giving her extra feed and cuddles.

"Poor girl, is he still giving you a hard time? He's a rotten, lousy dolphin, Bonnie... don't know how you put up with him."

Bonnie, as always, gave me soft eyes and pushed her head into my hands.

"You can't let him keep getting away with it, girl. He's been at you for over a week now... you must do something."

Clyde watched us, furiously glaring from the far side of the pool.

A generated anger pervaded the air – anger so strong I could actually feel it. The dolphin radio was seething, but the signals were crossed.

Was it simply down to Clyde, or was Bonnie in the mix?

There was no way of knowing. Either way, a force was building, intensifying – a vengeful wraith emerging to consume the entire pool.

My plan was working... I was convinced.

Stage side, I returned Clyde's glare.

"You'd better start watching your step, Clyde, or you might just get a nasty surprise!"

Giving Bonnie one last hug, I threw him a cool glance, then strode offstage.

In the kitchen, I found Vance gloomily preparing another batch of fish. "What's this for?"

"Backhouse wants another pound of flesh," he grumbled, "an extra show. Seems a coachload of people have just arrived, all wanting to see a dolphin. You never get a break in this bloody place..."

"Really?" I smiled. "That *is* good news."

Vance raised his eyebrows. "Good news...? Good news for who?"

"Good news for us, with any luck. Clyde's cruising for a bruising and I've got a feeling that today is the day."

Not just a vain hope, either. Something inside was literally yelling, "It's gonna happen!" In fact, the feeling was so overwhelming that I had another word in Vance's ear just before going onstage. "You'll have to be at the top of your game this show, Vance, because, I'm telling you, Bonnie's gonna 'ave him!"

He gave me a conspiratorial smirk. "Are you sure?"

"Oh, I'm sure... something's gonna give."

❦ 11 ❧

As soon as the show started, Clyde resumed hostilities. When he and Bonnie returned to the stage after their opening bows, instead of rising by her side to take his feed, he barged her out of the way, wagging his head and shrieking.

"*Shut your mouth, Clyde,*" I countered, "*and leave Bonnie alone... I'm warning you...*"

"*YOU warning ME?*" Clyde growled. "*You and whose army?*"

"*Right, I've had enough of you... no fish... no nothing until you learn to behave!*"

Clyde glared at me.

"*So what?*"

So what indeed! He didn't care about fish. This wasn't about fish anymore; this was about putting me in my place. But in his eagerness to humiliate me, neither did he realise just how close to the edge he was skating. Hopefully, he was heading for one mighty fall.

Up to now, Bonnie has tolerated his nastiness only because her patience would stretch to one show – but I strongly doubted whether it would stretch to two. She was a hair's breadth away from snapping – I could see it in her eyes. All she needed was a bit more egging-on.

"*Don't let him get away with this, Bonnie. Put your foot down – preferably on his head!*"

He heard that one all right... now he was baring his teeth... snarling at me...

Well, tough!

As the show progressed, Clyde's venom reached frenzied heights. Blinded by rage, he nose-butted and bit Bonnie with such ferocity that I could no longer stand idly by. The situation was getting dangerously out of hand and I had to do something – fast! I tried dropping the good girl/bad boy tactics – not just for Bonnie's sake, but for that of the audience, which was growing ever more edgy.

"You're a lousy dolphin, Clyde, a rotten, lousy dolphin…"

So left with no other choice, I bowed to pressure and begrudgingly reinstated his feed – only to have him fling it back at me.

"Keep your rotten, filthy fish – I don't want it!"

I stood on the poolside, stunned, whilst Vance repeatedly apologised to the audience for Clyde's behaviour. With a sinking heart, I had to accept that my gamble had failed: Clyde had won the battle.

Crestfallen, I looked into Bonnie's eyes…

… there was a change.

Somewhere deep within, a fire had flared, hot and menacing.

"Why are you feeding him when he keeps hitting me? Why?"

"I'm sorry, Bonnie, I'm sorry… I have no choice… we can't go on like this…"

"WHY ARE YOU FEEDING HIM?"

The valve was about to blow…

… outrage…

… sheer, unmitigated outrage.

I could feel it bubbling…

… a white-hot fury searing the inside of my head.

By giving Clyde fish, I'd unwittingly pushed Bonnie over the edge, plummeting her headlong into an abyss of rage.

However, a gloating Clyde failed to sense the change. Drunk with power, he persisted in thrashing his head and punching her with his snout.

"I'm the boss now," he screamed, *"I say what goes – not him!"* Then, as if to reinforce the point, he drew back his head and smashed Bonnie's face so viciously as to knock her fully sideways.

She reeled as the sickening thud echoed throughout the dolphinarium…

For a moment, my heart stopped beating…

… "*Bonnie… Bonnie…*"

Time froze. She hung motionless in the water, eyes squeezed shut with pain; then, gradually, deliberately, she opened them to look directly at me…

… rage… pure, unadulterated rage.

Slowly, she began to turn towards him, head ratcheting with taut and deliberate precision, bull neck cranking around in short jerks like the second hand of a clock…

… clunk… click… clunk… click…

… a Victorian wind-up toy.

Their eyes met and Clyde instinctively shied back, his entire body visibly stiffening as he realised with horror that he'd just overstepped the mark.

Terrified, he fled… fled from the stage to cower in the corner of the pool – ironically, the same corner where he'd so cruelly deposited poor Herb'e after attacking him.

Clunk… click… clunk… click…

Bonnie's formidable bulk swivelled around to follow him, zooming-in on its hapless target; then her powerful tail thundered down, launching her through the water like a rocket.

"*Go on, Bonnie – do him!*"

Clyde cringed with absolute dread as she hurtled towards him – and I swear, if he could have physically climbed out of the pool, he would have.

The water parted, then bubbled like a cauldron as Bonnie hit him full on. I could see her powerful tail scything through the froth and foam. The only other thing visible in the mêlée was Clyde's flailing head…

I'd never before heard a dolphin scream, but that's exactly what Clyde did.

As an appalled audience looked on, Vance, voice breaking with alarm, whispered, "She's gonna kill him! What do we do?"

"Nothing," I replied, "we do nothing."

Clyde's shrieks brought a panicking Tommy racing from his office – The Lone Ranger to the rescue!

Galloping purposefully down the auditorium steps, he reached the pool's edge only to dither uncertainly, a look of abject horror on his face. Nothing he could do. Nothing anyone could do, but listen to Clyde's squeals of anguish echoing around the pool.

Tommy gave me a pleading look, so I beamed Bonnie another message of encouragement.

"Go on, Bonnie – do him good! He's asked for it!"

The agonising reprisal continued on for a full four minutes before Bonnie finally withdrew, returning to the stage with a look of pure satisfaction on her face.

Kneeling down, I put my arms around her neck and hugged her close.

"Well done, Bonnie – that showed him! I bet you feel a lot better now, don't you? After that performance, I think you deserve an extra special treat!"

She beamed gleefully as I emptied the entire contents of the fish bucket into her generous mouth.

The conflict was over, but, alas, so was the show, because the wounded Clyde remained sulking in the corner of the pool with his back to the stage and his face pressed up against the wall.

"That's it, Vance, show's over. We won't be seeing him again for a while."

Smiling, Vance lifted the microphone to his mouth. "Due to a matrimonial difference of opinion between our two stars, we are unable to continue the show. Sorry, folks, but that's the way it goes sometimes."

I laughed to myself – that had to be the understatement of the year.

Waltzing offstage and into the kitchen, I literally glowed. Tonight, for the first time in ages, I would be able to free my dolphins into the main pool without fearing for their safety, because Clyde would be in no fit state to inflict any further damage... for the time being, at least. This bully had at last met his Waterloo, and it would take him some considerable time to recover from his public humiliation.

Today, my gentle giant had gotten me out of gaol.

"Well done, Bonnie… sweet dreams."

❦ 12 ❧

The boom arrived as promised, allowing me to pen Bonnie and Clyde.

Clyde had been remarkably quiet since his thumping, although how long he'd remain that way was anybody's guess. I'd won the battle, but not the war, and didn't doubt that he'd eventually rally. In the meantime, I was at last free to work my dolphins in relative peace.

Releasing them from their imposed incarceration had yielded rich rewards. They worked with renewed vigour – Baby and Scouse on the back somersault, and Duchess and Herb'e on the body spin or 'corkscrew', as it was sometimes called.

Observers had reported seeing spinning dolphins in the wild but, to my knowledge, no one in Britain had ever trained this spectacular trick. It would prove a worthy fill-in before work started on the jewel in the crown – the double forward somersault.

Although the water was still deteriorating, I managed to maintain it to some extent by pouring neat chlorine down the sumps, where it mixed-in via the filters. This procedure was risky, as it was liable to create chlorine clouds that could potentially burn the dolphins, but I had to try to avoid clashing with Tommy.

That would come soon enough when I would eventually be forced to dump the pool without his consent.

❧ 13 ❧

A full month passed before Tommy next called me into the office. "The shows at West Coast have collapsed," he snapped, "so we need you to go down there and put them right."

I couldn't believe what I was hearing. "That's Gerry's pool – why do you need me?"

"Gerry's gone sick and no one's been able to contact him."

"What about Sally? She's at West Coast. Surely she can sort it?"

Tommy answered abruptly. "If you're referring to Miss Summers, she's no longer in the employ of the Company. West Coast doesn't need – and certainly can't afford – two trainers."

I was flabbergasted. "When did she leave?"

His expression remained impassive. "Doesn't matter – she's gone and that's an end to it."

I struggled to take in what he was saying. I couldn't believe so much had happened without my hearing about it: Sally gone and Gerry missing. But one thing was certain: Gerry would eventually return and, when he did, he wouldn't take kindly to my being in *his* pool.

"Look, Tommy, if you force me to go to West Coast, it will cause ructions. It's Gerry's baby and he won't like me interfering."

"Well, Gerry's not there and the Company's losing money, so we have no choice. I want you there by tomorrow at the latest."

I reluctantly agreed, but at a price. West Coast must accept a gift: two grumpy penguins – a fitting recompense for Gerry having foisted them on me in the first place.

Tommy immediately agreed. "I think that's a very good idea," he said, brightening, "it's about time someone else put up with them. Besides, they'll prove a welcome distraction from the failing shows."

So, early next morning, I set out for the West Coast pool accompanied by the pungent Smelly and Worse. On arriving, I found no one at home, so freed the penguins, then settled myself into the kitchen to read the logs – diaries which should tell me just what the resident dolphins could and could not do.

I'd been sitting there for about thirty minutes when two male presenters nonchalantly rolled in. On seeing me, they stopped short. "Who are you?"

"I'm David Capello from the Hendle pool. Tommy Backhouse has sent me to bring your shows back online."

They stared at me blankly.

"I'm told the shows have collapsed," I added. "Is that true?"

Both men seemed nonplussed. "I suppose they have…"

Clearly, Management hadn't informed them of its decision to call me in, and I guessed they were feeling resentful of what they deemed to be an invasion of Gerry's territory. Well, tough, I wasn't happy either – I had enough problems of my own without inheriting any of theirs.

Reluctantly, the two presenters followed my orders to prepare buckets full of fish. Meanwhile, I continued to plough through the logs. As expected, these confirmed that Gerry was indeed having difficulties. Firstly, there was a water problem – so nothing new there. But, more worryingly, his dolphins didn't seem to be making any worthwhile progress. They were well behind in their schedules, which meant I'd have a lot of catching up to do.

Although these dolphins were new to me, handling them wasn't a problem as I was familiar with Gerry's training procedures. Throughout that first day, I worked continuously – forty-five-minute sessions followed by thirty-minute breaks – the same tactics I'd used during those early days at North Liston.

All training took place under the scrutiny of a distrustful dolphinarium staff. No one uttered a word unless questioned. You could literally cut the air with a knife.

For three full days, I struggled to rally totally disinterested dolphins and, slowly but surely, my efforts began to pay off. They blossomed, proving that all they'd ever needed was a little care and attention.

By day four, my success had gained me celebrity status and I found myself unexpectedly surrounded by a clutch of converted presenters, all teeming with questions. Taking advantage of my sudden popularity, I enquired as to how Gerry had come to book sick, and was told that he'd been complaining about severe headaches and the pressure of work – symptoms that were all too familiar.

Gerry had been suffering from exhaustion and – with Sally gone – there had been no one qualified to take up the slack. Management had chosen the cheaper option of replacing a qualified trainer with a presenter – someone who'd probably never even seen a real dolphin, let alone worked one. Yet, stupid as I believed this to be, I didn't dare comment – I couldn't afford to get involved in West Coast politics. I was in enough trouble as it was. I might have rescued Gerry's show, but Gerry was still Company head trainer and he would view my visit as a humiliation. I'd be a fool not to expect repercussions.

But my stint here had imbued me with renewed confidence, and now I was determined to confront Tommy about dumping the Hendle water, which was bound to have deteriorated even further during my absence.

And if he refused?

I'd take my chances and dump anyway… whether he liked it or not.

❦ 14 ❦

On my return to Hendle, I was greeted by a relieved Vance. It seemed that, during my short absence, Clyde had reverted to his bullying ways and was once more busily intimidating my two dolphin teams. He'd even had the front to start menacing Bonnie again. Even worse, the pool smelt like a sewer and all dolphins were showing signs of skin flaking.

I immediately pressed Tommy for permission to do a partial water dump, but again he refused. I could keep silent no longer.

"Tommy, look at the state of the dolphins. We must dump."

"You know Company policy on ditching water," he barked. "We'll just have to work on higher chlorine levels to get by."

"We can't work on higher chlorine levels – they're high enough as it is. It's not about 'getting by' anymore."

But Tommy was immovable. "You know how the Company feels about this. Under no circumstances will I allow any dumping of water – and that's final!"

It was pointless arguing. He'd made it abundantly clear that he wasn't for turning. Nevertheless, before leaving his office, I couldn't resist firing a parting shot. "Tommy, you can't keep hiding behind some misguided Company policy. The filters aren't up to it – they're second-hand and, even worse, they were never meant to deal with dolphins in the first place. I know you don't want to upset Head Office, but maybe it's about time you did, because they're not the ones having to work here… we are."

Tommy remained pokerfaced, silently busying himself with the suddenly pressing task of rearranging his desk files.

I'd obviously been dismissed and, realising this, I turned, dejectedly closing the office door behind me. Tommy had left us with no choice – when he left for home that evening, Vance and I would spring into action.

❦ 15 ❧

"Right, mate, he's gone, so let's get this done! Lock the doors, then join me in the filter room."

Vance grinned with delight. "Now you're talking – and about time, too!"

In a matter of minutes, the backwash had started and the pool was slowly emptying. I gave my partner-in-crime a smug smile. "Well, we've pulled the plug and now there's no turning back."

"Yeah," Vance chinked, eyes sparkling with schoolboy mischief. "Backhouse would go ballistic if he knew."

I planned to perform only a partial ditch, giving us valuable time to refill the pool before morning, hopefully leaving Tommy none the wiser.

"It's gonna be another all-nighter, Vance," I warned. "We'll be fit for nothing tomorrow."

Vance shrugged. "Well, let's make the best of it, because Backhouse is no fool and I have an awful feeling that he's onto us. Let's just hope we're finished before he gets in."

I shook my head. "It's gonna be tight."

"Well, tight or not, he's left us with no choice."

Vance was right, but we were still committing a barefaced act of disobedience and, if Tommy caught us, we'd be in serious trouble.

As usual, Sod's Law prevailed and, next morning, Tommy arrived much earlier than expected. On entering the pool room, he couldn't fail to miss the low waterline and immediately realised what we'd done.

Face flushing with anger, he glared at me and waved a forbidding finger. "Office... now!"

Within minutes, I'd received a verbal warning – nothing less than I expected. But I was shocked rigid when he called Vance into the office and issued him with one as well. It was grossly unfair, as Vance had only been obeying my orders, but Tommy had seized this opportunity to demonstrate what would happen to anyone daring to follow my lead.

And it didn't end there...

Still on the warpath, he immediately called a staff meeting. "From now on, all workers must be out of the building by six-thirty pm – with no exceptions. Last night, a flagrant abuse of trust was committed and I have no intention of allowing it to be repeated."

I cringed. His new directive would effectively end my all-important somersault training. "What about night training?" I complained. "It's the only time I have to get new tricks."

"You should have thought about that before you disobeyed me," he replied tersely. "You've brought this on yourself."

At last, Backhouse was showing his true colours. Moreover, he'd officially thrown down the gauntlet, little suspecting how keen I was to pick it up.

From now on, battle lines were being drawn, because I would not allow him or anyone else to interfere with my somersault training... whatever the consequences.

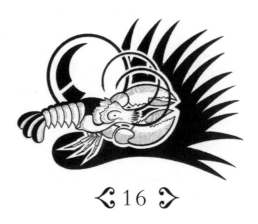

16

It took the best part of a week before Backhouse and I engaged in any meaningful conversation and, even then, we only spoke when necessary. Nevertheless, for me, this was a price worth paying: since the dump, all my dolphins seemed genuinely happier and – more importantly – healthier. Even the grumpy Clyde wore a sunnier disposition.

My main worry now was for Vance, because Backhouse was targeting him at every opportunity, making me realise that if I stepped out of line again, Vance might be the one to pay the price. Nevertheless, I still wasn't prepared to take Backhouse's heavy-handedness lying down. I was about to start fighting back.

I called my staff into the kitchen.

"Right, boys and girls, time for a team talk. From now on, come what may, we must all strictly adhere to Backhouse's six-thirty pm finishing time. Unfortunately, this means no training, no playtime, no cleaning… in fact, no anything after six-thirty pm. This especially holds true for the Monday and Thursday fish deliveries, which normally take place between seven-thirty and eight o'clock – something our esteemed general manager has obviously overlooked.

"Under no circumstances does anyone wait behind to accept these deliveries. Any late night packing of fish into freezers now falls to him." I smiled. "He can't complain, because we are only following his directive – something he holds dear to his heart. Hopefully, this should give him a gentle reminder that more than one can play at his game."

I was right: it didn't take Backhouse long to realise that a commercial dolphinarium couldn't function without staff flexibility, and within ten days, he had permanently – albeit begrudgingly – rescinded his directive.

Round one to the good guys.

Backhouse was visibly seething at having to back down, but nonetheless needed to tread carefully. He might be general manager, but he still had to answer to the main man, Rogers – someone who held me in high regard.

During this period of unrest, the park itself remained quiet. However, we were still performing two shows a day, and it was during one of Baby and Scouse's performances that Vance's enthusiasm again got the better of him.

Part way through a performance, we always invited some lucky kid onstage to take a boat ride. After that, they'd be asked to referee a football match where the dolphins would knock balls into the auditorium using their tails. This was always a popular routine, because anyone catching a ball could keep it.

Today was no different and it wasn't long before we were joined by an eager birthday-boy, keen to get a closer look at the dolphins.

"Hello, my friend, what's your name?" Vance asked.

The boy spoke shyly into the mic. "Andrew."

"Well, Andrew," Vance grinned, "we don't usually do this, but as a special birthday treat, we're going to give you a chance to swim with our dolphins. Would you like that?"

Andrew's eyes grew luminous. "Yeah, that sounds great!"

Giving me a wink, Vance gently nudged him towards the pool. "Right, go on then… in you go!"

This was actually a normal part of Vance's routine, and the kid usually responded to his nudge by leaping back nervously.

But today, we were in for a shock: without hesitation, a fully clothed Andrew dived in.

I cringed. "Oh God, Vance, nooooo… not another disaster!"

The audience gasped with shock as Andrew disappeared beneath the water's surface, then burst into relieved laughter and applause as he re-emerged, waving vigorously.

Ever cool, Vance simply raised his eyebrows and flashed a smile.

"Now, folks, you didn't expect to see that today, did you? No rush, Andrew... take your time... have fun!"

A stunned Baby and Scouse didn't share Vance's enthusiasm, however. They swam to the edges of the pool, point blankly refusing to even acknowledge the young intruder who, in their eyes, had tried to jump on them. After several minutes of trying to attract their attention, a disappointed Andrew finally gave up and swam back to the stage.

"Right, our kid, out you come," Vance smirked. "We can't have you catching pneumonia or your mum'll kill us."

Dragging himself onto the stage, Andrew took a quick bow before disappearing into the kitchen to dry off. But, unfortunately, the unexpected event brought the show to a premature end, as Baby and Scouse fell into a sulk and refused to finish their performance.

"Sorry about this, folks," Vance quipped. "Baby and Scouse obviously can't stand the competition. Looks like the show's over..."

What we couldn't have known, however, was that a local newspaper reporter happened to be sitting in the auditorium, meaning we inadvertently made the late edition. The newspaper's headline read, *Andrew goes swimming with the dolphins*, and the story finished with, 'Vance and Dave are now re-scripting'. What the reporter forgot to add were the words '...yet again'. Still, I had to laugh – life was never boring with Vance around.

So ended another of our many shared adventures – and I hoped there'd be plenty more.

But these were uncertain times, and I couldn't shake the feeling that our partnership was living on borrowed time.

❧ 17 ❧

A full month passed and my relationship with Backhouse was back on track – almost friendly, even.

Unfortunately, I couldn't say the same for Gerry. Communications with West Coast had ceased altogether, confirming my fear that he'd viewed my rescue mission as a personal insult – especially humiliating because I'd once been his student. Still, on a happier note, Gerry's return meant that West Coast was no longer my problem... or so I thought, until Backhouse made a shocking revelation.

"David, I need you back at West Coast. I've had a telephone call from the manager, Clive Rothwell – he wants rid of Smelly and Worse ASAP. It seems everyone's sick and tired of being bitten and cleaning up after them."

I smiled cynically. "Well, there's a surprise. That didn't take long, did it? I bet this is Gerry's doing...?"

Backhouse's expression became impassive. "No... not Gerry... Gerry's gone."

"Gone?" I was stunned. "Gone where?"

"He's no longer with the Company."

"No longer with the Company? Why, what happened?"

"Doesn't matter – the only thing that matters is he's gone."

Backhouse, his expression studied and blank, categorically refused to elaborate.

But I couldn't leave it there. I was finding it particularly hard to believe that Gerry could leave without so much as a goodbye call – or, for that matter, that he could leave at all. Surely, he hadn't resigned? He'd enjoyed huge popularity at West Coast and Clive Rothwell would never have let him go willingly, meaning Head Office had to be involved. If this was the case, authorisation to get rid of him could only have come from Rogers himself.

"Gerry is Europe's top trainer," I pressed, "so why has the Company allowed him to go?"

Realising that I wasn't prepared to let him off the hook, Backhouse begrudgingly replied, "Gerry Mansell is *not* Europe's top trainer – not any more. *We've* got Europe's top trainer here at Hendle, so Mansell is surplus to requirements."

"Europe's top trainer here at Hendle?" His words hit me like a hammer blow. "Me? Do you mean *me*? Are you telling me that *I've* replaced Gerry as Company head trainer?"

"Yes... why not? You've achieved far more in your short time with us than he ever did. He was just an expensive commodity."

I was flabbergasted. For me, this was a huge compliment – especially coming from Backhouse – and I should have felt immensely proud. But I didn't. Instead, I felt sad and disturbed, as if I'd somehow been used as a pawn in a corporate chess game.

I already knew that Gerry and Backhouse shared a chequered history and never spoke. But I had a strong feeling that there was more to Gerry's removal than met the eye. With Gerry gone, Backhouse had effectively been elevated to second in command, answerable only to Rogers himself. Now, as Rogers' right-hand man, Backhouse would have unrivalled power over Company policy, effectively making him the new face of the dolphin project.

For Backhouse, this could only be described as a fortuitous development, begging the question, was my 'promotion' indeed in recognition of my achievements, or was it simply part of a Backhouse plot to remove his main rival? Either way, this now meant that I wasn't just the Company's *head* trainer, I was its *only* trainer, as all other employees were presenters.

"Who's replacing Gerry as trainer at West Coast?" I demanded.

"No one," Backhouse tersely replied. "The Company doesn't

need trainers – the dolphins are already trained. We need only presenters."

I felt my jaw begin to tighten. "Doesn't work like that, Tommy. You need a qualified trainer to keep both dolphins *and* presenters up to scratch."

Backhouse, as always, was quick to reply. "Trainers are an expense we can well do without. Besides, let's face it, anyone with a whistle and a fish bucket can train a dolphin."

His comment snatched my breath. "What... what did you say?" I snapped. "You've got to be joking! Not only is that an insult, but it's an outstandingly presumptuous remark coming from someone who's never trained a dolphin!"

Backhouse flinched visibly – that last remark had certainly hit the spot – and, without uttering another word, he turned sharply and marched out of the kitchen.

However, our conversation left me deeply troubled. Was this just Backhouse's personal opinion or had he brainwashed Head Office into thinking the same way? Either way, when something eventually went wrong – which it would – I'd be the only person left qualified to put it right. A huge responsibility.

As for Gerry, I couldn't believe that Management had treated him so callously. I'd lost my friend and mentor without even getting a chance to say goodbye – yet another solemn reminder of just how cut-throat this business could be.

❧ 18 ❧

It was hard to accept that Gerry was gone. I could still hear his warning ringing in my ears: "One day, Backhouse will knife you in the back." I was convinced that this is what he'd done to Gerry, and couldn't help but wonder who would be next.

And now, to add insult to injury, I was expected to go back to Gerry's old pool to collect Smelly and Worse – something I wasn't looking forward to. The welcome would be frosty, to say the least, so the sooner it was over and done, the better.

"Vance, we've got to go to West Coast – Smelly and Worse are causing problems."

"Why, are they dead?" he quipped.

"No, worse than that – they're coming back here! The West Coast gang are sick of mopping up after them and, from what I can gather, they've had a go at someone."

"Oh, so West Coast hasn't improved their sunny dispositions, then?" he grinned.

It was about four in the afternoon when we arrived at the seaside dolphinarium, again to find the doors unlocked and nobody home. The place was in disarray, with props strewn across walkways and dirty fish buckets stacked in sinks.

"Just look at the state of it, Vance," I moaned. "This place is filthy, absolutely filthy. The handlers here need a good kick up the arse, and that's exactly what they'd get – if they had a trainer."

Before embarking on a search for the penguins, I couldn't resist glancing through the scantily completed logbooks, but learned only that the show was again on the verge of collapse. We then continued to hang around for a good ten minutes longer before a presenter finally decided to grace us with his presence – someone I didn't recognise, as it seemed that all staff loyal to Gerry had long since walked.

"Hi, I'm David Capello and this is Vance Martin. We've driven down from Hendle to relieve you of Smelly and Worse. You don't by any chance know where they are, do you?"

The presenter looked perplexed. "Smelly and Worse? Who's Smelly and Worse when they're at home?"

That's all I needed – a smart-arsed kid. "Penguins… I'm talking about penguins…"

"Oh, they're around here somewhere," he replied sullenly.

"Well, don't put yourself out!" I snapped. "I s'pose we'll have to find them ourselves." To be truthful, a task that wasn't difficult – we simply followed a snail trail of penguin dirt around the deserted auditorium, only to find the dastardly duo standing in their now customary pool of shit. On spying us, Smelly and Worse immediately adopted attack mode, wobbling towards us, flippers flaring, snapping and cawing.

"God, nothing changes, does it?" I grinned. "Good to see you, too!" I turned to the young presenter. "We'll need their cage. Where is it?"

"Cage?"

"Yes, cage… you know, the kind of thing you carry penguins in…"

He looked at me through heavy-lidded eyes. "Somewhere…"

"Somewhere? Somewhere where?"

"I don't know," he drawled. "Somewhere…"

"Well, we can't take them without their cage, can we? So go and find it!"

This presenter was seriously getting on my nerves and I was fast losing my rag. It was growing late and we had a long drive back to Hendle. But, after searching for the missing cage for another hour, we began to get desperate. Then, in a flash of inspiration, Vance came up with one of his infamous brainwaves.

"Look, Dave, we're gonna be here all night trying to find this bloody cage. Why don't we use cardboard boxes instead? That way, they can't shit all over your car seats. All we need to do is cut two holes in the lids for their heads to pop out." He broke into a triumphant smile, obviously wallowing in his own brilliance.

"Cardboard boxes…? Two holes…? I don't know about that…"

"Well, if we don't, we're not gonna get back to Hendle this side of midnight. What have we got to lose? I mean, we can't go back without them, can we?"

As usual, I wasn't convinced – but he had a point… we couldn't leave empty handed. So, after another twenty minutes of searching, we finally succeeded in unearthing two abandoned crisps boxes and set about cutting holes in the lids.

"There, that'll do nicely," Vance assured me, putting down the scissors. "Jobs a good 'un!"

"I'm still not sure about this, Vance," I replied apprehensively. "It just sounds like another exercise in blood-letting to me."

"Oh, ye of little faith! Don't worry, it'll work, believe me…"

I shrugged. "Okay, but I'm still not sure…"

Wrapping torn towels around our hands and arms for protection, we set about capturing the renegade Smelly and Worse.

"Right, Vance, I'll hold the box and you stuff them in – but don't mess about, otherwise we'll end up cut to pieces!"

Getting the two birds inside the boxes was like getting square pegs into round holes. Vance grasped the first penguin with outstretched arms, pinning its flippers to its wriggling body, goading it into slashing at his hands and arms.

"Aaargh! Bloody hell!"

"Come on, Vance, stop messing about!"

"God, the vicious little bugger's just took a chunk out of me…"

The dolphinarium echoed to a further five-minute barrage of colourful language before Vance finally mastered the battle-weary Worse.

"It's amazing how something so small can be so feisty, isn't it, Vance?"

My flippant observation met with stony silence as he tentatively removed the blood-stained towel that had meant to be protecting his hands. Gritting his teeth, he glared at the raging, open-mouthed penguin and snarled, "Lousy, rotten, vicious little bastard!"

Trying unsuccessfully to suppress a grin, I gave him a sympathetic pat on the back. "Well, that wasn't so bad, Vance... was it? One down, one to go. I'll keep an eye on Worse while you go and get Smelly."

"What do you mean, 'go and get Smelly'? It's your turn!" Vance wailed.

"I don't take a 'turn', Vance, I'm the boss... I'm Company head trainer. Besides, I've got to hold the box, haven't I? And I can't do everything...!"

Following a further chaotic ten minutes, a shredded Vance finally succeeded in stuffing Smelly into the second box.

Mission accomplished. All that remained visible of the angry penguins were two snapping, squawking heads – beaks wide, eyes like sulphur. Boy, were they hacked off!

Within minutes, I was throwing towels over the back seat of my car. "I'm not taking any chances. Those two pump out battery acid and the last thing I need is all their rotten crap leaking onto my leather seats." Giving Vance an apologetic look, I added, "I'm sorry, Vance, but you'll have to ride with them in the back to make sure the boxes don't fall over."

"So, what if they do fall over? What difference does it make?"

"A big difference," I growled. "If they get out, it'll be pandemonium back there, which is the last thing we want."

It was gone seven before we eventually pulled away from West Coast with the two grumpy penguins persistently pecking at poor Vance. It was going to be a long journey home for him. Feeling just a little guilty, I endeavoured to lift his spirits.

"Are you all right back there, Vance?"

"No, I'm bloody well not!"

"Well, chin up, nearly there..."

It was gone ten by the time we arrived at Hendle, only to find that it had been raining heavily, flooding the grass verges alongside the road. Throughout the entire horrendous journey, the foul stench emanating from the back seats was overpowering, with both penguins adding to the discomfort by squawking relentlessly. The only thing loud enough to drown out their racket was Vance's ceaseless whining. He never shut up moaning… I don't know how I stood it…

"Bloody rotten things… I'm bleeding to death back here…"

Then, to add to my woes, on approaching the main gates of the safari park, I suddenly realised that I'd forgotten to inform security that we'd need access to the dolphinarium during the night.

"Vance," I said innocently, "I hope you remembered to tell security that we need to get into the dolphinarium tonight…"

"No, I thought you'd done it," a harassed Vance replied.

I sighed loudly, but made no comment. Yet another problem to raise its ugly head. No way could we take the penguins back to our digs, but neither could we leave them in the car all night. One way or another, we had to get inside the park.

"Shit, if you don't get me out of the back of this car quick, I'm gonna need a blood transfusion…"

Twelve-foot-high wrought iron gates barred our way, crisply silhouetted against a full moon. The park was otherwise in total darkness, and we had no idea how to contact security. After a few minutes pondering, I made a suggestion.

"Vance, there's only one way to get in. We'll have to climb over the gates."

"What? Climb over the gates? Are you mad? Look at the height of the bloody things!"

"It's no good grumbling – it's the only way… unless you fancy sleeping with *them* tonight?"

He didn't answer.

"Good, so that's decided, then. Right, over you go!"

"*Me*? Why me?" he wailed.

"Because I need to be on this side so I can throw them over while you catch them."

"Why can't *I* throw them over and you catch them?"

"Because, as I've already explained, I'm the boss – Company head trainer… Plus, it's my idea."

Begrudgingly, Vance began his laborious climb, inching his way upwards with every grunt, puff and grumble. "I don't bloody believe this... it's not fair!"

"When you're over, I'll throw the first box and you catch it," I shouted after him.

I visualised that throwing the box would be like tossing the caber – the only sure way to keep it upright. The penguin was heavy, so this would require some considerable strength and technique. Not a brilliant plan, in retrospect, but all I could think of at the time. Neither of us would have been able to make the climb carrying a boxed penguin and, even if we could have, we'd have been totally lacerated by the time we reached the other side. So it was muck or nettles, as the saying goes.

"Are you there, yet?"

A tearing sound as Vance's tee shirt became another casualty of our daring enterprise.

"Sod it!"

"Get on with it, Vance, we haven't got all night."

A heavy splosh signalled that he'd landed on the other side.

"Are you ready?" I shouted.

"Ready as I'll ever be," he muttered.

As I grasped the first box, I noticed that the base was damp and spongy due to what Smelly and Worse did best. We'd made it just in the nick of time. I shouted a warning to Vance.

"Here it comes! Now, make sure you catch it – we don't want the penguin landing on its head."

Muffled grumbling.

"I know... I know... just do it!"

The penguin wasn't making things any easier, taking chunks out of my hand at every opportunity. A final excruciating bite kick-started my run-up. One, two, three... release.

"Heads up, Vance... he's on his way...!"

The boxed penguin sailed over the gate, briefly silhouetted against the moon before disappearing into the darkness.

A thump... a grunt... a groan... followed by the sound of a triumphant Vance. "Got it... got the little sod!"

The irate bird immediately rewarded him with a slash of its razor-sharp bill.

"Aaargh... bloody thing...!"

I couldn't believe it – amazingly, my hastily thought-up plan seemed to be working. One more to go...

I picked up the second box, which was even more sodden than the first – in fact, pretty near to disintegrating. I couldn't delay any longer. It was now or never.

"Okay, Vance, are you ready? Here it comes!"

A short run-up, then release. The box sailed upwards... up... up... up.... And I watched with baited breath, willing its journey, its every twist and turn.

Then, the dreadful truth began to dawn – due to the box's sogginess, I'd misjudged its weight and grossly underthrown.

The spikes on top of the gate snagged at its base, ripping it apart, and I watched in horror as the dark silhouette of a penguin – minus box – sailed across the moon before plummeting into the blackness towards an unsuspecting Vance.

As luck would have it, directly behind the gate was a small area of scrubland, thick with foliage. I heard a heavy squelch as the penguin catapulted over Vance's head and into the lush undergrowth.

"Quick, Vance, don't let it get away or we'll never find it in the dark!" I screamed.

All I could hear were the muffled sounds of my partner frantically rooting through vegetation. "I can't see it... I can't see it... where's the bloody thing gone?"

Hurriedly and clumsily, I climbed the gate to give him a hand. Time was of the essence and, much as I disliked the penguins, I didn't fancy having to explain to Backhouse how I'd managed to lose one. I was over the gate in minutes, desperately grubbing around in the undergrowth.

"Got it!" Vance cried, triumphantly lifting the groggy Worse like a trophy. "Got the little bastard!"

Good old Vance, for a minute there I thought we'd lost it.

However, the nightmare didn't end there: we spent another fifteen fraught minutes stumbling down the moonlit path before finally arriving at the dolphinarium, where we quickly and thankfully gave Smelly and Worse their freedom.

The penguins waddled away grumpily, seemingly unaffected by their ordeal.

Alas, the same couldn't be said for Vance and me. Clothes torn, arms and hands bleeding, we sloped into the kitchen to begin the painful task of cleaning and dressing our wounds.

"Thank God you found that penguin, Vance," I sighed. "I hate to think what would have happened if it had got into the lion reserve."

"Yeah, me too -" Vance growled, "them lions wouldn't have stood a chance!"

❧ 19 ❧

As the weeks passed, the position of head penguin keeper once again fell to poor Beryl, the deck scrubber she'd thought redundant now constantly in her hand. "I'm fed up cleaning after these two. This was never a part of my job description."

As always, I feigned deafness.

On a brighter note, training was going fantastically well – especially with Baby and Scouse, whose back somersault was now close at hand. The speed of their progress was hard to believe, as it seemed like only yesterday when Vance and I had spent all our time improvising as these two little misfits struggled to entertain. But no more. My dream of owning two top dolphin teams was firmly back on schedule.

And the good news didn't end there: Duchess and Herb'e were making rapid headway with the body spins – another exclusive looming – unbelievable progress considering the problems caused by Bonnie and Clyde. Thank goodness for the boom.

However, one downside: Welby Park pool was now behind schedule, which meant that Bonnie and Clyde wouldn't be leaving any time soon. Their planned three-month stay at Hendle had now been extended to six.

One morning, whilst sifting through the dolphinarium mail, I noticed an envelope postmarked from Germany and addressed to me. This was unusual, as my post normally consisted of letters from local fans and wannabe trainers.

"Who can this be?" I muttered, eagerly tearing open the envelope,

"I don't know anyone from Germany." But my excitement soon changed to shock: it was from Gerry's partner, accusing me of stabbing Gerry in the back and conspiring with Backhouse to steal his position as Company head trainer. She'd written several pages, lengthy, rambling and bigoted, and slating me to such a degree that I deemed them unworthy of a reply. I was ambitious – true – but Gerry had been special to me and this accusation was grossly unfair. Deeply hurt, I re-sealed the envelope and marked it *return to sender.*

Wounded and disillusioned, I decided to press Backhouse for some much-needed leave. I hadn't had a day off since my breakdown and desperately needed a change of scenery – plus, I wanted to make new props for the stage, which was looking decidedly shabby. The materials I needed were back in my dad's City workshop, giving me the perfect excuse to return home.

An unusually accommodating Backhouse agreed to give me fourteen days to complete the work, so early next morning I set off to spend some quality time with my family. After all, we were only doing three shows a day and had six dolphins to perform them.

What could possibly go wrong?

❧ 20 ❧

It felt great to be with my family again, living like a normal teenager and taking time out to practise my art. I painted two boards, each displaying a coat of arms bearing the legend 'Duchess and Flippa' and flanked by two leaping dolphins – a truly fitting tribute to my two stars.

These displays took ten days of intense yet enjoyable work to complete, and proved to be a welcome break from the stresses of the dolphinarium. By the time I'd packed away my paints and brushes, I still had four days of freedom to look forward to... but when the telephone rang later that evening, I instinctively knew that my leave was over. A clearly agitated Backhouse urgently needed me back at the pool where problems had developed with all six dolphins.

As I walked into the dolphinarium the next morning, I was greeted by a harassed Vance.

"Boy, am I glad to see you! Duchess and Herb'e have packed in work, we've got major problems with Clyde and that rat Backhouse has been giving me hell."

I sighed – so much for peace and harmony! "Well, to be honest, Vance, I'm not surprised about Duchess and Herb'e – you know they won't work for long without me. But what's all this with Clyde and Backhouse?"

"Where do you want me to begin?" he whined. "It's been like Casey's Court around here. For starters, Clyde's found a way to escape the boom. During one of the shows last week, he got out and attacked Baby and Scouse. He's made a right mess of them... they're both badly marked."

"Escaped the boom? How's he managed that? It's too heavy to move... Surely he didn't jump it?"

"No, he didn't jump it, he got *around* it!"

"Around it?" I stared at him in disbelief. "You've got to be kidding! How?"

"He managed to find a weak spot where it doesn't sit flush against the wall, so when Bonnie leans against it, he can wriggle through the gap."

"Bonnie leans against it? You mean Bonnie's actually helping him to escape?"

"Well, you can't blame her – she probably wants rid of him, like everyone else." He shook his head in bewilderment. "But here's the best bit: guess who's Clyde's new best mate?"

"Not Backhouse?" I gasped.

"No, that bastard hasn't got any mates." He looked at me pointedly. "It's Herb'e."

"Herb'e?" I laughed. "Never! Not in a million years!"

"Well it is! They're a gang of two, swimming around together, causing mayhem. And – can you credit it? – Backhouse actually thinks it's *my* fault! We had a blinding row in which he accused me of dumping water again on the sly... so I told him a few home truths."

I cringed. Vance and Backhouse had obviously been at loggerheads for the full ten days, and Backhouse didn't need any excuses. This was the last thing I needed – my friend had played right into Backhouse's hands.

"That rotten bastard hasn't got a clue," Vance persisted. "He's all top show – playing the big shot – but he's ignorant, totally ignorant. He's nothing but a snake in the grass!"

I raised my hands. "All right, Vance, all right... I get the point. I know it's hard, but just try to keep the peace while I get things sorted." I glanced up towards Backhouse's office. Door firmly closed, he clearly wasn't for coming out, which was disturbing in itself.

The rest of the morning crawled by, the atmosphere menacing. Vance was still visibly uptight so, to give him a break, I asked one of the girls to join me for the afternoon Baby and Scouse show. It was then that I witnessed Bonnie and Clyde's teamwork first-hand.

Painful as it was incredible, I watched in amazement as Bonnie deliberately pressed her considerable weight against the bottom of the boom, allowing a wriggling Clyde to make his escape.

But then, to my horror, once in the main pool, he immediately launched a brutal sexual attack on Baby.

"No... Clyde... no... leave him alone!"

Clyde mounted the tiny dolphin, digging his teeth deep into his back. Baby raced around the pool, screaming in terror as he desperately tried to escape Clyde's clutches.

"No you don't... not this time, Clyde... I'm not having it... and I don't care about the audience!"

I swung around to grab the hurdle-pole... but, amazingly, Scouse was already on the job, powering his way to the infant's rescue and forcibly ramming the gangster dolphin off his back.

A terrified Baby fled to the corner of the pool as an enraged Clyde turned on Scouse. The water erupted as the two dolphins clashed.

Being blind and much smaller than Clyde, this was a fight Scouse couldn't possibly win, yet the courageous little dolphin didn't roll over and capitulate. He fought on pure instinct, meeting Clyde's challenges head-on, bravely defending his little friend. Each time Clyde knocked him down, Scouse got right back up – he was certainly one tough little number.

Eventually, however, my tiny prizefighter had no choice but to yield, leaving a jubilant Clyde to celebrate his victory at the foot of the stage.

"You bastard, Clyde!"

Leering at me from the water, he responded by again activating that dark, silent *connection* – cold, probing and intimidating. Then, cocking his head, he dismissively left the stage to swim to Herb'e's pen.

"See, he's not in control – I am."

Clyde was once more in pursuit of pool domination. But this clever dolphin had learned a valuable lesson from our last encounter. Now, instead of challenging me directly, he was employing stealth specifically designed to generate anarchy within the ranks... with Herb'e being his first convert.

Once the distraught audience had left, brave Scouse came to me for comfort.

"Poor old lad… what's he done to you? The rotten, lousy sod!"

He was badly marked – but, equally, so was Clyde. Clyde might still be top dog, but I had a feeling he wouldn't be challenging Scouse for a rematch any time soon. My feisty dolphin had unquestionably earned Clyde's respect.

As I was examining Scouse's injuries more closely, I suddenly heard a door slam, followed by the heavy footsteps of Vance racing down the auditorium stairs. He'd exploded from Backhouse's office, white-faced and fraught – and I instinctively knew what was coming.

"He's sacked me!" Vance screamed, struggling to control his anger. "Shithouse has sacked me!"

"Sacked you? Sacked you… why?"

"For telling the scheming rat the truth about himself, that's why. And, what's more, the devious sod's purposely waited till you got back before doing it."

My heart plummeted – not just for Vance's sake, but also for my own. For me, Vance's dismissal would be nothing short of crippling. Since our arrival at Hendle, he'd been my crutch, buffering my fragile psyche against the anxieties of running the dolphinarium. Without him, I'd never be able to cope.

I galloped up the auditorium steps to Backhouse's office where I pleaded for Vance's reinstatement. He had extensive experience, I argued, exceptional skills honed in the harsh breaking pens of North Liston. But it was no use, Backhouse didn't value experience – for him, anyone with this commodity posed a threat to his own ambition. Besides, Backhouse knew all too well that in getting rid of Vance, he was effectively cutting off my right arm, leaving me more vulnerable than ever.

Nevertheless, he still allowed me to grovel on my friend's behalf, extracting his pound of flesh and enjoying the spectacle in the process.

With an air of superiority, Backhouse swung around on his chair. "I don't see what the problem is. Vance can easily be replaced. People like him are ten a penny. After all," he added coolly, "anyone with a whistle and a fish bucket can train a dolphin."

❦ 21 ❧

That evening, as he packed his few belongings into a battered suitcase, I begrudgingly said goodbye to my unsung hero. With Vance gone, I was no longer able to afford the flat, so was forced to give notice to JMR. My 'promotion' to Company head trainer had not yet yielded any financial reward and I was desperately short of money. In this respect, the conniving Backhouse had been more than happy to exploit my devotion to my dolphins.

The sacking of Vance again reminded me that no one was indispensable – not even me. Of the original North Liston team, I was now the only one remaining, anyone with any experience having been systematically removed – a calculated manoeuvre that Backhouse had executed with flawless precision.

However, having handed my notice to JMR, I now needed somewhere else to stay, so placed an advert in the local newspaper seeking 'lodgings in a friendly family environment'. As if by magic, I received a call the very same day and arranged a viewing for later that evening.

Not surprisingly, the atmosphere between Backhouse and me had become very tense. However, unable to run the pool with one man down, I had no choice but to confront him about recruitment.

He responded in his usual supercilious manner. "A number of rookie presenters will be joining us next week. Most of these will eventually be destined for Welby Park. Unfortunately, none of them have any stagecraft, so it'll be down to you to teach them."

Now I knew why Backhouse had been so accommodating when I'd asked for leave – he'd already recruited Vance's replacement. It seemed that my friend's dismissal was not as off-the-cuff as Backhouse had wanted me to believe. He was indeed that snake in the grass that Vance had so colourfully described.

"What about a trainer for Welby Park?" I enquired.

"Welby Park doesn't need a trainer – Bonnie and Clyde are already trained."

Backhouse's snappy answer only reinforced my earlier suspicions – he'd convinced a gullible Rogers that the Company no longer needed trainers.

"By the way, you already know one of the new trainees – it's Carol Swan, the student of Marine Biology. I presume you have no objections to working with her?"

I raised my eyebrows. "Would it make any difference if I did?"

No reply – Backhouse just stuck his nose in the air and dismissively turned away.

So, on top of all my other problems, I could expect to be saddled with the lippy Carol, who didn't even like me. Great… things were going from bad to worse.

Still, on a positive note, this might be welcome news for Beryl because, if the haughty Carol stepped out of line, she'd find herself replacing Beryl as nursemaid to Smelly and Worse – a thought that for some reason filled me with twisted delight. Either way, if Miss High-and-Mighty even looked at me the wrong way, it'd be my pleasure to introduce her to our dastardly duo… personally.

❦ 22 ❧

We still had two days to go before the new recruits were due to start work and, with Vance sacked and one presenter sick, we were effectively two staff members down.

Being already familiar with Bonnie and Clyde, Backhouse astonishingly offered to present their show whilst I compèred. Something I readily agreed to – not just because I needed the help, but also because I was curious to see how he would cope.

He surprised me by handling the performances adequately, albeit sloppily. Clearly, once upon a time, he'd been taught to present. Still, I couldn't shake the feeling that this sudden desire to help was more about proving to me that he, too, could work a dolphin.

As always, he was choosing to overlook the difference between a presenter and a trainer, ignoring the crucial fact that a presenter merely demonstrated the results of a trainer's vision and hard slog. Still, to someone as top-show as Backhouse, this was a subtlety best ignored.

After the show, believing he'd proven his point, he quickly disappeared back into his office, leaving me to release the dolphins from the pens on my own.

Because of Clyde, my customary training sessions had again become impossible. His ability to escape the boom had effectively turned back the clock, forcing me to abandon training altogether. I was falling further and further behind in my work schedules, so organising alterations to the boom's structure was of paramount importance.

Herb'e's bonding with Clyde was replicating dolphin behaviour in the wild, where an adolescent male would instinctively seek the adventure of a boy gang. However, it also meant that Duchess and Bonnie were now doomed to swim alone during playtimes – a development that risked destroying my dream of *The Perfect Pair*. So the sooner Clyde was gone from the pool, the better.

Another peculiarity was how Scouse had taken on the role of Baby's bodyguard, deliberately shepherding him away from Clyde. My little prizefighter clearly had no intention of allowing the gangster dolphin to repeat his assault on the infant – although, in truth, he needn't have worried. A canny Clyde exhibited no desire for a second showdown with what he evidently deemed to be a formidable opponent.

My fascination with blind Scouse had developed almost as quickly as my love for him – although, no doubt, he was an anomaly. No one had been able to determine his age. Was he young or was he old? I suspected old. Either way, he was certainly different from the other dolphins – almost uncouth, even. It was obvious that he didn't fit and would have been an outcast even in the wild, yet here he was enjoying a relationship with a dolphin too young to have learned prejudice. An ironic twist that, here in captivity, he had at last found acceptance – an acceptance he was happy to reciprocate. Baby had become Scouse's eyes, just as Scouse had become Baby's adoptive father. Two little dolphins who complemented each other perfectly.

Overall, my enchanted mirror reminded me of a giant soap opera with a hundred different plots slowly unfolding towards one dramatic conclusion. And, somewhere, buried deep within this kaleidoscope of mayhem, was its director – me – wrestling to orchestrate the desired outcome.

Having released the dolphins for the night, I set off to view my new digs and meet my prospective landlady. Carla was a petite brunette in her late forties; she had a radiant smile and it was impossible not to like her. Her home, which she shared with her two teenage sons, had an easy, comfortable feel to it – a perfect place to chill and undoubtedly the tonic I needed following the loss of Vance.

Carla's home was just what the doctor ordered and I couldn't wait to move in. Whatever else my problems, I knew I'd absolutely love it here.

❦ 23 ❧

An interesting morning as Backhouse introduced me to the six new trainees, five of whom were seeing a live dolphin for the first time. The sixth, of course, was the attractive but lippy Carol – the only recruit not destined for Welby Park. As always, our greeting was polite, but lacking warmth, and Carol's unease plainly matched my own as she struggled to broker a smile. Her sustained air of aloofness merely reaffirmed what I already knew – she didn't like me, which was going to make working together awkward. Still, I had enough on my plate without worrying about her, so I'd just have to make the best of it.

On a favourable note, I now had the unprecedented luxury of manpower on tap, so my first task was to add an extension to the base of the boom, making it far too heavy for the ingenious Bonnie and Clyde to manipulate. The extension took the form of a metal pole similar to those used in the boom's initial construction. My only problem was that I had to fit it underwater, which was time-consuming and necessitated the use of an Aqua-Lung.

As I worked from the pool floor, I was conscious of Clyde watching my every move.

"*I know you're there, Clyde. I can feel your eyes burning into my back.*"

Silence… just an eerie echo emanating from his cold *connection*.

"*You can watch me all you like, Clyde. Once I've fixed this pole, your goose is cooked, because this boom's going nowhere!*"

As he turned to swim away, a wave generated by his powerful tail slammed into my back, signalling that my scan was over. I couldn't resist a smug smile. He knew I was right – his Houdini act was over.

Meanwhile, Herb'e, Baby and Scouse hovered above me, playing in the bubbles from my Aqua-lung. Only Bonnie and Duchess stayed clear, deserted by their partners and swimming alone.

This was upsetting, as I'd hoped that my little princess would seek support from the mature Bonnie, but, surprisingly, both kept their distance. In fact, Bonnie became uncharacteristically aggressive whenever Duchess drew near – something I at first found hard to understand. Then, it dawned on me. Herb'e was becoming sexually mature, so it was logical to assume that the same might be happening to Duchess. If so, Bonnie would soon have a new love rival in the pool, which could mean more trouble on the horizon – a particularly frightening prospect. The last thing I wanted was for Bonnie to lock horns with Duchess – especially in light of what I'd seen her do to Clyde. I could only pray that her normally gentle nature prevailed.

It took me a full day to attach the heavy pole to the base of the boom – time well spent if it put an end to Clyde's escapades. With him out of the way, I would at last be able to resume training – the back somersault with Baby and Scouse and the body spins with Duchess and Herb'e. Until I'd established these tricks, I would not be able to begin work on the trick I coveted most – the forward somersault – or I would risk confusing my dolphins.

Hauling my tanks onto the poolside, I could still feel Clyde's icy scrutiny.

"You won't get out of there in a hurry," I repeated, coolly returning his gaze.

Eyes narrowing, he held his ground.

But I couldn't feel more satisfied. What a day! Firstly, I'd got one over on Clyde, and now I was about to give the best job at Hendle to a certain cocky female who needed taking down a peg or two.

The image was delightful: "Carol... say hello to Smelly and Worse!"

24

Almost a month had passed, and the reinforced boom had worked its magic, stopping Clyde from invading the main pool... but not, unfortunately, from causing chaos.

He persistently disrupted Duchess and Herb'e's performances by calling to Herb'e through the boom's mesh. Equally, during the Bonnie and Clyde shows, he spent most of his time with his nose pushed through the gates of Duchess and Herb'e's pen. Meanwhile, a gullible Herb'e fell completely under his spell, which meant I now had two adversaries to worry about instead of one.

Plus there was another concern: both Clyde and Herb'e were bullying their respective partners during shows – copycat behaviour – and I feared that if discipline continued to deteriorate I'd be forced to carry out a shake session – a practice I loathed.

I could only thank God for the ever-reliable Baby and Scouse, who, seemingly immune to Clyde's influence, relished the attention showered on them by the new presenters. This happy-go-lucky duo so continued to blossom that I decided to concentrate purely on their back somersault and cancel all further training with my *Perfect Pair*.

One evening, totally out of the blue, Carol surprised me by asking if she could stay behind to watch the Baby and Scouse training session – an almost friendly gesture which I found most refreshing.

"Yeah, okay," I smiled, "but only if you prepare the fish. But, be warned, you'll need to prepare a lot, because, with any luck, I'm gonna nail the back somersault tonight."

"Can I watch too?" A familiar voice called from the kitchen.

"Sure, Graham, you're always welcome. Help Carol prepare the fish, then lock the dolphinarium doors. I have a feeling tonight is gonna be special, so we don't want disturbing."

Not long afterwards, an overflowing fish bucket had materialised at my feet and I was ready to begin.

"All right, people, let's give you two little stars your own special!"

Back somersault, here we come!

❧ 25 ❧

I quickly bring my two little dolphins to order.

"We've got an audience this evening, lads, so let's give them something to remember."

The hairs on the back of my neck are prickling. I can literally feel Baby and Scouse's excitement... tonight they're incredibly receptive...

"This is the signal, Baby... look at the signal..."

I lightly tap my left shoulder twice with my right hand.

"Okay, Scouse, Baby's seen it... now it's your turn. Scan Baby... try to find the picture...look hard and concentrate..."

Scouse cocks his head to one side: my little prizefighter's having trouble tuning in.

"Can't find it... don't know what to do..."

"No rush, Scouse, just take your time. Me and Baby both have the image, all you have to do is find it."

I give Scouse a few more seconds before again bringing my tiny duo to attention.

"Are you ready, lads? Here's the signal, now... hold... hold... go!"

Both dolphins leap from the stage to perform an admirable half-back somersault.

Short whistle, small reward.

"Good, good... not bad at all! Nearly there..."

I repeat the signal: they enthusiastically make a carbon-copy performance.

Not good enough. Small reward, cuddle and thank you – but no whistle.

"Well done, lads, close... very, very close... but you need to go further. You need to let go."

I feel the impetuous infant scurrying about behind my eyes. Baby understands... he knows... he's seen the vision. Our minds lock: we exchange images of pure thought, mentally sharpening the picture.

"Baby, you've got to help Scouse. Remember, he can't see the signal with his eyes, so you have to prompt him. Are you ready?"

I make the signal.

"Go!"

Both shoot from the water. Scouse again rolls into a half-back somersault... but Baby performs a perfect one-and-a-half back flip.

"Yes, Baby! Yes... you've got it...you've got it!"

He enters the water to the sound of repeated whistles... and fish... lots and lots of fish.

"Superb, Baby, absolutely superb!"

Baby's got the trick and, even though Scouse hasn't, it's not a problem, because it's only a matter of time before the excited infant passes it on.

We're buzzing... all three of us buzzing... in the loop... and Baby's eyes are sparking anticipation...

Breathless... I feel Scouse's breathless *connection.*

"What's happened? What's going on? What have I missed?"

"Baby's got the trick, Scouse! We're just waiting for you, now. Try again... try to find the picture..."

Scouse rocks his head from side to side, probing for the link.

"That's it, Scouse, keep searching. It is there. You will find it. Right, lads, we're going one last time. Are you ready? Hold... hold... go!"

They jolt from the stage, cutting sideways through the water – not straight, but sideways, that's how eager they are. Seconds later, both are in the air. Scouse rolls into a three-quarters back somersault – *"Good boy!"* – but Baby executes a glorious two-and-a-half back flip. Magnificent!

Whistle – fish! Whistle – fish! Whistle – fish... continuous whistle – fish!

We've got it! We've got the somersault… and Baby is reeling with elation.

Poor Scouse – he's equally thrilled, but isn't sure why.

"What's going on, lads? Will someone please tell me what's going on…?"

"Don't worry, Scouse, Baby will tell you later. He'll show you the way – but for now, just enjoy…"

I empty the entire contents of the fish bucket into their open mouths.

Unbelievable! What a session! What a fantastic session! The atmosphere is charged: Carol is laughing, actually laughing… Graham is laughing… Baby and Scouse are laughing… I'm laughing…

… in fact, everyone's laughing…

Well, not quite everyone.

Other eyes watch… silent and resentful…

… from below the waterline, Clyde, hiding behind his boom…

… from above the waterline, Backhouse, hiding behind his office window…

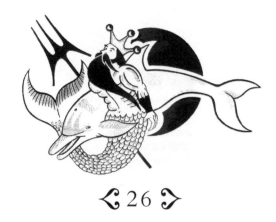

❦ 26 ❧

In less than three weeks, Baby and Scouse have added a glorious double two-and-a-half back somersault to their ever-growing trick list, elevating them to one of the country's top teams. They are now rubbing shoulders with the likes of Bonnie and Clyde. I can hardly believe it – it's fantastic! In fact, it's miraculous!

On the downside, I'm getting abnormal water readings – nothing too serious, but a painful indicator of things to come. Moreover, Backhouse has informed me that, due to another delay in the completion of Welby Park, the nightmare Clyde and his partner will be at Hendle for at least another two months – yet a further blow to my forward somersault training.

Thanks to Clyde, Herb'e's now as big a bully as he is, although nowhere near as aggressive. But all that could change and Duchess is no Bonnie – she's altogether gentler – so I can't expect her to do to Herb'e what Bonnie did to Clyde.

All in all, things are going from bad to worse and I'm now painfully aware that I'm losing control of the dolphinarium. I can no longer allow Clyde to dictate pool policy, so I must fight to bring Herb'e back into the fold, or there's every chance that I could lose him forever. Somehow, I must convince him to forget his new gang master and return to Duchess's side. I will not allow this gangster dolphin to kill my dream of *The Perfect Pair* – from now on the gloves are off.

I intend to remind Herb'e and Clyde just who's boss…

❧ 27 ❧

This unholy alliance between the manipulative Clyde and my gullible Herb'e continued to throw up ever more undesirable traits, the most annoying and embarrassing of these being a sudden upsurge in sexual activity. It seemed that Herb'e and Clyde now deemed any object – for want of a better word – 'screwable'. Herb'e, in particular, had developed an unnatural affinity for a blue and white plastic penguin, which I'd leave floating in the pool overnight. Other nocturnal playthings consisted of a giant toothbrush, a lifebelt and a hurdle – all previously insignificant objects that had suddenly taken on the mantle of sex toy.

Even Smelly and Worse weren't safe!

However, Herb'e's particular fascination with the manufactured penguin was bordering on obsession – something that didn't go down well with Duchess. Infuriated, she took every opportunity to toss her love rival out of the pool and out of Herb'e's reach – behaviour that I at first put down to frustration.

Although amusing to observe, I soon realised that this repeated act of sabotage went much deeper than a simple desire to spoil Herb'e's fun and games. Herb'e's XXX antics were attracting an ever-growing, open-mouthed audience – seriously ticking off my diva Duchess, who hated the thought of anyone stealing her limelight.

So fearing a prima donna style tantrum, I took the decision to confiscate the offending object for good – an act that clearly left Herb'e distraught. He trailed me around the poolside, staring at me with mournful eyes.

"Why have you done that, David? Why have you taken it away? You know I like it... why?"

"Look, Herb'e, I'm sorry, I really am, but I've got enough on my plate as it is without you antagonising Duchess."

But my half-hearted apology gave my mischievous dolphin little comfort and his never-ending sad-eyed assault left me feeling mean and guilty. Even so, I didn't dare restore the plastic temptress for fear of offending my temperamental princess.

"No, Herb'e, no," I told him with mock severity, *"I can't give you back the penguin. It's causing too much trouble. Girls aren't like boys... they don't understand these things!"*

But, alas, neither did my lovesick Herb'e who continued to mope around the pool, po-faced and miserable. So, in an effort to appease my tortured conscience, I waited until Duchess wasn't looking, then beamed him a covert message:

"Don't worry, Herb'e – it's not the end of the world. You might not have the penguin, but you've still got the giant toothbrush..."

clyde rules

❧ 28 ❧

Samo, samo… the opening spiel – a repetitive mishmash of words all melting into one verbal soup… horrible, absolutely horrible! Nevertheless, listening to it certainly conjured up some happy memories.

I have to smile. I can still feel the pat of his hand on my shoulder as he passes to walk onstage. Still hear that annoying comic phrase, "Another day, another dollar." What a case! What a comedian! What a friend!

Vance – I certainly miss him and can't help but wonder just what he's doing now. Still, he's gone and he's not coming back, and I've no time for reminiscing – particularly not this show, because Bonnie and Clyde are in the main pool and I've got a strange feeling that Clyde is cooking up something extra special for me today, meaning I'll have to keep my wits about me.

"Ladies and gentlemen, boys and girls, a big hand for your trainer, David Capello!" There's the applause. That's my cue. Another day, another dol… no, I can't say that… only *he* can say that. Either way, I'm on, so it's back into the fray.

"Hello, Bonnie, hello Clyde, are we up for this today?"

Good old Bonnie beams with joy, as always. Pity the same can't be said about Clyde, whose face is twisted with displeasure.

"Come on, Clyde, let's try and make it through at least one show without the usual hassle."

He's weighing me up, not saying anything, as always choosing to hide within his silent *connection*. But he's got something planned, something devious. I can feel it in my bones. Either way, can't dwell on it, because he and Bonnie are already in the air, signalling the start of the show proper.

"*Fantastic, Bonnie! Well done, Clyde! Three perfect opening bows. That should get the crowd going!*"

Bonnie's bubbling with excitement and Clyde... Clyde... well... he's... he's *smiling*... actually *smiling!*

I don't believe it! Clyde smiling...? Clyde never smiles – especially not at me! So why's he smiling now?

That isn't good... no, that isn't good at all...

"*What are you up to, Clyde? What are you planning?*"

Silence. Not a single word.

"*Still not talking, Clyde...? Well, there's a surprise...*"

Shape yourself, Capello. Concentrate. Next up is the handshake.

"*Okay, Bonnie – you first! Up you come! Hello, girl, how are we, today?*"

A shake of her flipper ends our introduction.

"*Good girl, Bonnie, nice to see you, too.*"

Next up is Clyde.

"*Hello, Clyde, glad to see me?*"

Great! He's not moving... not moving an inch. Just hanging in the water, giving me that assiduous stare from the foot of the stage.

"*Just what are you up to, Clyde?*"

No response, so I try again.

"*Come on, Clyde, it's too early in the show for you to start giving me grief. Move yourself...!*"

A compliant nod of the head.

"*Oh, that's a pleasant surprise... decided to work, have we? Up you come, then! Give me your flipper and... Oh no... OH NO... I don't believe it!*"

A leering Clyde rises out of the water, brazenly flashing me his manhood...

... I remain frozen, eyes bulging, gritting my teeth hard.

"*What's wrong? Don't you want to shake my flipper? Well, if you don't want to shake my flipper, shake THIS instead!*"

His squinting eyes spark belligerence, sheer belligerence.

"*God, Clyde, I hate you... I really, really hate you...*"

He smirks… smirks one of his infamous, supercilious smirks.

"You're supposed to be the big-shot trainer. What's wrong? Can't you hack it?"

I feel my face beginning to burn.

"Put it away, Clyde, or I'll give it a slap! I mean it… nobody wants to look at that measly little thing."

Clyde winces and jerks back his head in shock.

"Little? LITTLE? Who do YOU think YOU'RE calling little? YOU should be so lucky…"

I snap a glance at the red-faced compère. "He's really pushing his luck today," I hiss, "he really is… trying to show me up in front of all these people."

But Clyde's back is towards the audience, so no one in the auditorium has clocked his antics – at least not yet, although the feeble stuttering of my slack-jawed compère isn't helping matters.

"Stop gawking, girl, and pull yourself together. We need to get this show moving before Clyde gets anymore bright ideas!"

Yet another superior look from below.

"Any more bright ideas…? I'm full of 'em, sunshine! You don't get off the hook that easily."

I can feel his non-verbal message bouncing around my head. He's really enjoying this, revelling in my discomfort and taunting me about the chaos to come.

"Clyde, you're a rotten, lousy sod…!"

What's next…? Ring retrieval… God… I can already hear the cogs cranking in his brain… already feel the tug of his *connection* behind my eyes as he beams me a mental picture of what he's got planned…

I cringe.

"I HATE this dolphin… bloody HATE him!"

❧ 29 ❧

Got to stay cool... Can't let Clyde get to me... That's what he wants...
He wants me to lose my rag... In fact, he's banking on it...

*"I know your game, Clyde. You're trying to humiliate me in front of an
audience... in front of Herb'e. But it won't work – I'm not gonna fall for it."*

I hear the voice of the compère outside my head.

"Ladies and gentlemen, our next trick is a simple retrieval – one of
the first behaviours a show dolphin learns during its basic training. This
trick helps cement the bond between dolphin and trainer."

For God's sake, girl, give the flannel a rest and get on with it! All
you're doing is giving Clyde more time to think... more time to plan.

"Firstly, ladies and gentlemen, we ask our dolphins to hook a single
rubber ring on their nose, then bring it back to the stage. This done,
we make the trick a little more difficult by asking them to collect three
rings."

Got away with the first ring, but I won't get away with three. No
chance. This is where Clyde transfers his thoughts into action. This is
where he demonstrates his sheer contempt for me.

"There, boys and girls, see how Bonnie weaves the water as she
collects the rings. See how cleverly she hooks them over her nose. And,
Clyde, too, just look how he... he..."

She stops short – and no wonder!

"I knew you were gonna do that, Clyde, I just knew..."

I hear a voice from the audience. "Mummy, what's that dolphin
doing with those rings?"

She may well ask… what *is* that dolphin doing with those rings…? What an embarrassment!

"Dad? What's that sticking out of that dolphin?" little Billy demands loudly.

That's all we need – a little Billy in the audience. It's amazing how there's always a little Billy to point out the bloody obvious.

My blood is boiling, the silence in the auditorium is deafening and, as for my compère, she's lost her tongue altogether.

"For God's sake, girl, don't just stand there – say something!"

More stuttering. "Er… now… er… ladies and gentlemen… er… our two dolphins will now return the rings to their trainer."

Return the rings to their trainer…? *Return the rings to their trainer…?!* Good grief, this compère's got a lot to learn! Incredibly, she's made no comment about Clyde's antics… made no mention of how he's chosen to hook the three rubber rings with surgical precision on his… God, this is getting worse with every minute!

I stand onstage rigid with embarrassment whilst trying to maintain an air of authority.

Fat chance! How the hell do I do that? Even worse, how on earth do I get those rings back off Clyde? Especially with two hundred people looking on, all wondering exactly the same thing…

"What's wrong? You wanted me to bring back the rings. Well, here they are… so why don't you take 'em?"

I feel as though the stage is about to swallow me up. Now it's my turn to say nothing and hide in a silent *connection*. Even so, I've still got to get those bloody rings – and Clyde knows it.

So how do I do it? How? Do I make a quick grab… or… or… do I make a quick grab…?

… got to make a quick grab…

… a very, *very* quick grab!

Right… decision made!

The only way to avoid any further embarrassment is to move like greased lightning.

Two claps of my hands and both dolphins rise from the water to deliver their rings – Bonnie with her nose and Clyde with his you-know-what. But the rotten sod's not going to make this easy: he's purposely drifting just out of reach, meaning I'm having difficulty maintaining my balance.

"Come on, then, you want 'em, so take 'em! What's taking so long?"

A sharp intake of breath – it's now or never. Grimacing, I make a frantic lunge forward, but to no avail. The *connection* works both ways, and Clyde's ready for me, foiling my desperate smash and grab with a deft jerk backwards.

The sudden movement causes the rings to fall off and drift miserably on the water's surface.

The audience begins to titter… titter at the clever dolphin who's just made a fool of his big-shot trainer.

I squirm. So much for showing who's boss! Clyde's made a right spectacle of me today. His plan has worked. I've lost face – not only in front of an audience, but, more importantly, in front of Herb'e.

"You know, Clyde, at the risk of repeating myself, I really, really, REALLY DO HATE YOU!"

⧼ 30 ⧽

Clyde's embarrassing sexual broadsides continued fully for another week before he finally relented, no doubt deeming that this method of attack had lost its potential to shock. Nevertheless, I knew that this cessation of hostilities was only a respite: our game of thrones was far from over.

I was also aware that Clyde's recent success in humiliating me had given him the upper hand, weighing our power struggle firmly in his favour. We were now at a critical stage. For me, losing the next battle might mean losing the war, along with my all-consuming dream of the shadow ballet.

Surrendering the pool to Clyde was not an option. But, if I were to regain control, I would have to up my game, tactically switching from defence to offence…

… an offensive that would start today.

.

❦ 31 ❦

Today, our new recruits will enjoy a valuable first lesson in the art of
ad-libbing, because it will take some pretty fancy mic-work to gloss
over the chaos that's about to erupt during the shows.

Clyde and Herb'e are already plotting away through the boom,
Clyde no doubt giving his boy some last minute tips on how best to
disrupt the performance.

Herb'e is aware I'm watching, and lopes to the centre of the pool,
leaving Clyde to stare coldly at me from below the waterline.

"He's my boy now – not yours."

I throw him a dirty look.

"That's what you think, sunshine!"

I'm again fast losing my temper and the show hasn't even begun…
then, suddenly, I feel her calming influence and hear her hypnotic song
– Duchess, my lovely Duchess again drawing the sting. Of all my
dolphins, she is the one I love most – gentle, caring, compassionate.

"Hello, beautiful."

As I look into those bewitching eyes, I feel myself beginning to
smile. Kneeling, I gently cup her face – only to spy a fresh scar near her
blowhole. My blood runs cold.

"Oh no, is this Herb'e's work, Duch? Did he do this to you?"

She pushes her head into my chest, but says nothing. She won't make
trouble for her partner, won't drop Herb'e in it. She cares too much.

I glare at Herb'e, but he keeps his distance. He senses my pent-up
anger… and the battle to come.

87

"Bring it on, Herb'e."

I turn to the compère. "Listen, today isn't going to be easy," I tell him. "Today, I intend to discipline Herb'e in full view of the audience. I won't cut him any slack whatsoever, even if it spoils the performances. Every trick, every feed will be dealt with in a rigid and regimental manner. He's not getting away with anything... and I do mean *anything*. Do you understand?"

The compère nods nervously and, for the hundredth time, I can't help thinking how different it would be if Vance were here. This was the sort of challenge he'd revel in. But Vance isn't here and I have to learn to let go of the past.

I'm on my own.

"Right, are you ready?"

I call my dolphins to the stage, but Herb'e – deep in conversation with Clyde – refuses to take his place alongside Duchess. I wait, but he continues to ignore me, forcing me to start the show without him.

"Okay, Herb'e, if that's the way you want it."

I give the signal for the opening bows. An eager Duchess performs alone.

"Well done, girl, well done. We don't need him, do we?"

Whistle and double feed for Duchess.

Herb'e returns to the stage, obviously buoyed by Clyde's pep talk and all too willing to perform the much easier handshake. But, in so doing, he barges Duchess aside to steal her space.

"No you don't, Herb'e... I don't want to shake your flipper! Get lost! Do you hear me? Get lost!"

I crouch and shove him away. I feed Duchess, then – just to rub salt into the wound – I feed her again.

"Get back to Clyde, Herb'e – me and Duchess don't need you."

Herb'e didn't expect that, so swims to the foot of the boom for further instructions. I see Clyde egging him on, but cannot access their *connection*. They're hiding in a room I cannot enter. Yet, I'm aware that, at the same time as instructing Herb'e, Clyde is also probing my mind, groping for my next move. He's incredible, like a radio operating on two frequencies.

Herb'e's pep talk takes only seconds before he's back at the stage, head shaking, mouth open and abusing me loudly.

"Call me all you like, Herb'e… I'm not listening."

Now he wants to work. *Now* he wants to perform… but again without Duchess. He's driven her from the stage, and she's refusing to return, so I throw *his* reward to *her*.

"No intimidation, Herb'e… work with Duchess or not at all."

He remonstrates vigorously.

"Get lost, Herb'e!"

He jerks angrily from the stage, smashing his tail on the water before swimming to the corner of the pool to sulk – and it's obvious that he's not coming back.

With Herb'e gone, Duchess returns to complete the rest of the show alone. But, this time, I don't feed her as normal – I *double* her rewards and blow the whistle as loudly as I can, just to make sure that Herb'e knows what he's missing.

"Great this, isn't it, Duchess? All this fish, just for you!"

Herb'e smoulders in the corner.

"That's right, Herb'e, bugger off and stay out of our way… like I said, we don't need you!"

Boy, is he throwing a tantrum! But he's not the only one: from behind the boom, I feel Clyde's angry glare. This hasn't gone quite the way he expected and he's livid, absolutely livid!

GOOD!

❧ 32 ❧

The last four performances have been hell, the psychic battles leaving me mentally and physically drained. I'll be glad when the day is done. Nevertheless, I daren't give in. I've got to keep going.

Herb'e's still sulking in the corner, refusing to return to the stage unless I give in to his demands… or rather, *Clyde's* demands. Well, no chance.

"Stay in your corner and sulk, Herb'e! I've had enough of you!"

I lavish Duchess with ever more attention to show my appreciation for all her hard work.

"Thanks, girl. Herb'e's a bad boy, isn't he?"

Again, I cup her face, and she rolls into my arms.

My mind offensive is working – I've successfully initiated the Herb'e shut-out. He's now lost his partner.

Today, in the hope of breaking Herb'e, I've breached all the rules by allowing Duchess to perform solo. However, I can't continue this strategy for long or Duchess might start to exploit the situation by intentionally pushing Herb'e out. This is now a delicate balancing act, so it's imperative that I win him back quickly or I may lose my dream team forever.

In the meantime, I assure my new recruits that I have no intention of backing down. "If it takes a day, a week, or even a month, I will win. This is a fight I cannot afford to lose. And if Backhouse – or anyone else, for that matter – doesn't approve, well that's tough!"

Tonight, I'm absolutely shattered, so have decided to give Baby and Scouse's training session a miss. Instead, I release all dolphins into the main pool and invite everyone to take part in the playtime swim.

As expected, Clyde immediately swims to Herb'e to give him moral support. After all, his boy's had a bad day… and he'll be having a few more if I have anything to do with it.

As I sit cleaning my facemask on the poolside, Duchess nibbles playfully at my toes.

"I'm coming, girl. Give me a minute to get organised."

Once I'm in the water, she pushes her head under my arm, rolling onto her back so I can tickle under her flippers.

"Ooh, that's lovely, isn't it, Duch?"

With Herb'e in disgrace, Duchess now has me all to herself – something Herb'e will hate. I am conscious that he's watching from the corner as Duchess and I play together, so I press my advantage.

"Hey, look, Herb'e, I'm pinching your girl."

He looks on in silence.

The mind games continue.

I've already given everyone strict instructions not to pet either Herb'e or Clyde under any circumstances, and I can feel Herb'e's pain as he misses out on our games. I notice how he tentatively manoeuvres towards us in the hope of joining in, so I chase him away.

"Go on, Herb'e, get lost… told you before, we don't need you!"

I'm beginning to get to him. He's hurt and upset, but I mustn't weaken. I have to stay strong. It's the only way to bring him back into the fold. He has to learn that he can't have it both ways.

Then, suddenly, Herb'e's *connection* dissipates and I sense, hidden within the water current, a liquid shift – a deep-seated frustration. I become creepily aware that this exercise is no longer about breaking Herb'e's will. It's about something else… something altogether darker…

My alarm bells go ballistic…

… from the corner of my eye, I see him.

Underwater, Clyde is circling menacingly, watching me through narrowed, malevolent eyes. He reminds me of a python, ringing his prey. His icy *connection* targets me, filling me with foreboding and I can practically hear the machinations of his mind. He can't stand it any longer, can't stand not getting his own way.

I've pushed him too far.

Squeezing my swimming space to a minimum, this dark destroyer tightens his grip.

I'm in *his* element.

Vulnerable… and he knows it.

This is his chance: he's thinking about challenging me… actually, seriously thinking about challenging me…

… but the *connection* works both ways and I'm ready.

"Come on, Clyde… it's me and you… always has been…"

He despises me, reviles me, but the feeling is mutual. Our eyes lock and we both drift motionless beneath the water's surface, bodies upright and rigid: two combatants frozen in time. He's psyching me out, waiting for me to flinch.

My breathing becomes shallow as mere seconds turn into an age, but I cannot move… dare not move. I cannot afford to even blink. All I can do is… wait.

My eyes begin to bulge as the pressure behind them intensifies.

I clock his every move, every twitch.

Mentally, I draw a line around the contours of his body.

Abruptly, his powerful tail flicks, propelling him sideways and to my left, and my heart skips a beat.

In tandem, I follow suit, pushing to my right so that we remain facing each other. I continue to fix him with my stare, scrutinising him for the tiniest muscle tremor, the slightest shift in position, whilst all the time, the belligerence of his smirk embraces our stalemate and his silence slices through me like a knife.

"How far are you prepared to go, Clyde? How far are you willing to push it?"

A guttural rattle penetrates the liquid amphitheatre as my psychic message smashes home. He bares his razor sharp teeth before exploding into violent head shakes. Clyde's just upped the ante, taken it to a new level. He's initiated DEFCON 2.

I feel the force of his hostility, sense his breath piercing the waveform

and pushing into my face. Truly frightening, yet I cannot back down…
not now… I *cannot* back down…

Biting on my mouthpiece, I imitate his threat.

"Come on, sunshine, I'm waiting."

He contemplates his next move.

Like a physical force, I can actually feel his thoughts churning.

The sound of his rattle intensifies.

I freeze.

My God, he's going for it… he's actually going for it… he's going
to attack…!

My ribcage balloons with a violent intake of air.

"You dare, Clyde, just you dare…"

A torrent of blood punches the back of my eyes as I hunch my
shoulders and clench my fists. I'm fully pumped up. My body's about
to explode…

Everything goes into freeze-frame…

… time stops…

… I am deaf…

… I no longer hear the sound of his rattle…

… I no longer hear anything at all…

Then, suddenly, unexpectedly, his cold aura dissipates and the
speakers switch back on.

Contemptuously, he turns aside.

I breathe again.

He knows better. Like all bullies, he won't go that final mile.

Today, I win the battle – the battle, but not the war.

But tomorrow is another day. Bring it on!

❦ 33 ❧

Cocooned in the maternal embrace of an easy chair, all my aches and pains melted away, the shriek of the training whistle but a memory. Yet I was all too aware that, even in the retreat of Carla's home, the art of peaceful contemplation was a goal I had yet to master.

My troubled mind was again replaying the vivid events of yesterday. It was hard to imagine that just eighteen hours earlier, I'd literally been dancing with the devil. Only now was I coming to terms with just how lucky I'd been.

Crafty Clyde was a super-intelligent and powerful dolphin, and if he'd made good his threat of attack, there could only have been one winner. Yet another debt of gratitude owed to my guardian angel.

This had been Clyde's first foray into physical confrontation – something I had to ensure didn't happen again. Yesterday's events had left me very much aware that time was my enemy, driving home the message that I had to win back Herb'e quickly or lose him forever. Somehow, I needed to reconnect a mind dialogue with my wayward dolphin, bypassing the corruptive link he shared with Clyde.

"Come back to me, Herb'e... please come back! You belong to me... you always have..."

After a good breakfast, I arrived at the dolphinarium feeling determined and renewed. Not so the presenters. Following last evening's swim, they were agitated and complaining of itchy skin – a sure sign that the water was turning. We needed a partial ditch, but that was a two-man job and there was no one here I could trust to assist me. My esteemed general manager had seen to that.

Although Backhouse had regularly helped me to perform short backwashes, they were merely damage limitation exercises and nowhere near sufficient. For now, I could do nothing but again alert him to the deteriorating water situation and log my concerns in the diaries.

Flicking through the pages, I couldn't help but watch Carol as she meticulously wrote up the previous day's events in her notebook. This was something she'd done every day since joining the payroll, important observations supposed to help her in her studies. Instead, she was clearly becoming ever more confused by the behaviour of my dolphins.

Sensing her vulnerability, I seized my chance. "You're deep in thought, Carol. How's it going?"

She sighed. "Working here has turned everything I ever thought I knew about dolphins on its head."

I smiled reassuringly. "Welcome to the real world, Carol. If it all gets a bit too much, I've got a straitjacket going spare that should just about fit you."

Glancing up, she beamed me a warm smile... a truly rare thing. Maybe, just maybe, my ice-maiden was finally melting.

On a serious note, however, my off-the-cuff joke couldn't help but remind me of Gerry's comment: "Dolphinariums don't just break dolphins – they break people, too." Odd, because I'd always believed that Gerry was thinking of me when he'd made that remark, never realising that in fact he'd been talking about himself. Sad, really – I'd never guessed just how similar we were, because, even after all this time, I was still finding it hard to cope with dolphinarium life without the help of my Valium.

❧ 34 ❧

It's the first show of the day and we have over two hundred expectant punters in the auditorium. Duchess and Herb'e are in the main pool, so armed with my trusty whistle, I steel myself in preparation for the mental battle to come.

I brief the compère. "Hope you slept well last night, because you'll need to have your wits about you today. I'm expecting trouble again. You already know the drill – I'm not allowing Herb'e to get away with anything. I must break him. Understand?"

He nods.

"Right, out you go!"

As I listen to his opening spiel, my mind conjures the image of a Master of Ceremonies introducing the Big Fight – a comparison that the normal Joe-in-the-street might find a tad extreme. Yet the importance of this show cannot be understated.

I stride into the ring to be greeted by Duchess' smiling face. But Herb'e is again noticeable by his absence, chatting to Clyde through the boom – a final pep talk from his manager before fitting his gum-shield.

Right, round one!

I edge to the poolside and try to attract his attention.

"Come on, Herb'e, get your skates on… it's show time."

I meet his gaze just below the waterline, where he drifts hesitantly as if unsure what to do next.

Is he wobbling, or what?

I sense a change… an inner conflict…

Maybe this is the chance I've been waiting for. If I can hook him into performing the opening bows with Duchess, it's game on. But, I have to catch him early… give him no time to think…

The compère's opening introduction seems to last for an age. "Come on, hurry it up… we need to get this show on the road!"

I give the signal for the opening bows, but no one moves – not even Duchess. She looks at Herb'e expectantly, delivering an ultimatum:

"Are you with me, or not?"

Good old Duch – she's applying pressure, helping me out.

I feel a raging conflict of mind… something's happening…

My breathing suspends…

… time stands agonisingly still…

… he's wobbling… he's definitely wobbling…

"Come on, Herb'e, you can do it!"

Still, no movement.

"Come on, come on…!"

Herb'e returns Duchess' gaze and a message passes between them… a transmission I cannot access, beamed from a secret place…

Duchess receives and processes the data…

… then they both turn to look up at me.

"Come on, people, come on! What are you waiting for?"

The trauma of inner battle again hits me. Herb'e is still wrestling with himself. I feel the strain behind my eyes as my mind locks on to his, gripping it in a psychic vice.

"Stay with me, Herb'e, stay with me!"

I cannot allow Clyde's message to reach him… got to keep swamping Clyde's signal…

"Come on, Herb'e, you can do it… stay with me… you must stay with me…"

My head is exploding. A star field blurs my vision.

"Come on… come on…!"

Pressure… pressure… can't hold him any longer…

"Go!"

My thought explodes like a bullet from a gun barrel…

... BANG!

Within seconds, *both* dolphins are flying through the air, performing three glorious opening bows.

Thank God, I've got the start I wanted!

My pain is blown away.

"Yes, that's it, people... that's the way!"

A prolonged, noisy whistle and I shower them with fish and excited banter.

"Great people... great! Good boy, Herb'e! See what you've been missing?"

The air's electric and Herb'e's buzzing, flinging open the doors to his mind. The psychic energy that he's generating almost knocks me off my feet. Fantastic, absolutely fantastic! But I can't take any risks... got to keep talking... got to keep drowning out Clyde's signal...

"Yes, Herb'e, yes... you're such a good boy... such a good a boy!"

He's shaking his head and his mouth is wide open − not in remonstration, but in joy, sheer joy at being welcomed back into the team. But he's not the only one: Duchess is bouncing, too, eyes sparking fire, ecstatic to have her partner back.

"Yes, Herb'e, yes... Isn't this good? Isn't this great?"

Herb'e's now well and truly back in the mix. But I still can't give him time to think... got to keep talking...keep him away from Clyde.

We're not there yet...

"Yes, yes, did you enjoy that, Herb'e? Well, did you? Come on, did you?"

He's wagging his head in utter delight. He can't wait to perform the next trick.

Then, I suddenly become aware.

"I can hear you, Herb'e, I can HEAR you. You're talking again... you're talking!"

Duchess and Herb'e are fit to burst with an enthusiasm that's infectious. I feel their energy coursing through my body.

"Yes, people, yes... it's just like old times! We're back, we're back!"

Fabulous... and although this may not be our best show, it's undoubtedly our most momentous.

Less than thirty minutes later, a long blast on my whistle signals an end to this epic performance. My team is at last restored to me, but I still can't rest on my laurels. I have a further three shows in which to cement our renewed bond and wipe Clyde's influence away forever.

Today, me and Duch have broken Clyde's hex and won back our friend. What a feeling – what a glorious, glorious, wonderful feeling!

But, as elated as I am, I know there will be a price to pay for my psychic bombardment. Today, my inner light has burned twice as brightly and, by the day's end, I am bound to be suffering from burnout. Still, I'll worry about that later, because all that matters now is the result.

What a comeback! Despite all Clyde's planning, all Clyde's deceptions, I've ridden out the storm, leaving his dream of pool domination in tatters.

Clyde's not only lost the battle, he's lost the war… and he's not happy… not happy at all.

And neither is Bonnie, God bless her, because, whether she likes it or not, Duchess isn't the only one to get her partner back.

Poor Bonnie – she has my deepest sympathies.

❦ 35 ❧

As the season progressed, we were soon delivering six shows a day and, with most of the staff shortly due to leave for Welby, Backhouse was finally forced to hire Vance's replacement.

This came in the shape of Dan Conner, a shy and thoughtful ex-school teacher. His appearance was noticeably striking: straight, black hair and slim figure, giving him a Vulcan-like appearance reminiscent of *Star Trek*'s Mr Spock. In fact, the resemblance was so uncanny, I felt as if we were already old friends.

"If you're thinking of saying, 'Beam me up, Mr Scott!' I want your autograph before you go," I quipped.

Dan obviously got the joke and laughed loudly – very un-Vulcan-like behaviour.

As we got to know each other, Dan admitted that this was the first time he'd ever encountered a live dolphin, further reinforcing my belief that Backhouse was purposely avoiding hiring anyone with experience – a policy that couldn't be down to cost-cutting alone. It screamed of something altogether more sinister – a fact I was ruminating on when the man himself summoned me to his office.

"The West Coast shows have collapsed again and Clive Rothwell needs help getting them up and running. He wants you down there as soon as possible."

I raised my eyebrows. "He's actually asking for *me*?"

"There's no one else."

"Well, I *know* that, but last time I went to West Coast, they made

Reflections From

FLIPPA   DUCHESS

The Mirror

A smiling Bonnie – the gentle giant!

Bonnie and Clyde beaching at Welby Park Dolphinarium

Bonnie and Clyde at Hendle Dolphinarium – a magnificent beaching with tails held high!

Bonnie and Clyde – the gangster duo

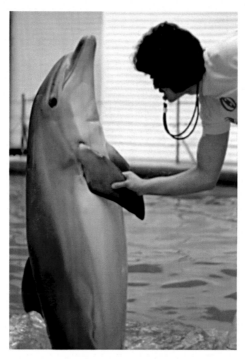

Hello Herb'e, how are you today?

Duchess watches Capello's every move

Vance presents a uniform show feed to Duchess and Herb'e

Vance gets to know a young Duchess and Herb'e

Dan says 'Good morning' to Duchess

Duchess and Herb'e's spectacular body spins – the second
movement of the shadow ballet

Capello in his nightmare filter room

The breathtaking double backward tail walk

Coat of arms and logbooks… from another era

Duchess and my bundle of mischief – eager to work

Capello makes for a head catch

Capello struggling with the less desirable option of a tail catch

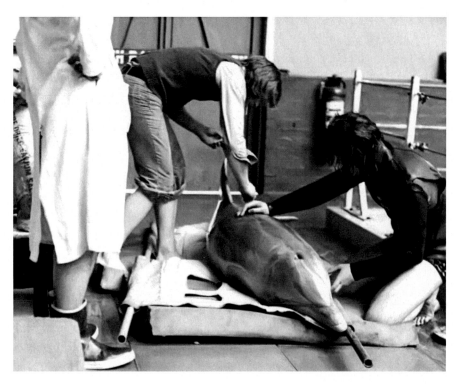

A veterinary examination following a catch

An exhausted Capello after catching Scouse –
note Scouse's battered dorsal fin

A truly beautiful photograph – Duchess and Capello

A gourmet banquet of herring and mackerel!

Carol presenting the double hurdle with Duchess and Herb'e

it blatantly clear that they didn't like me interfering. Things must be bad…"

"Well beggars can't be choosers," Backhouse snapped. "They're in the middle of the holiday season and losing money, so you'll have to go."

He didn't leave me much choice so, despite my misgivings, I agreed to set off early next morning.

The West Coast dolphinarium adjoined a prominent show bar, The Kentuckian, which attracted some of the biggest cabaret acts in the country. Just opposite was the huge amusement park, Fun City. All three venues fell under the Company umbrella. However, their managers originated from the fairground fraternity, so had no experience of dealing with dolphins.

On arriving, I was met by a completely new batch of presenters, all the old faces again having moved on. Nevertheless, the customary West Coast distrust was as strong as ever.

"Hi, I'm David Capello from the Hendle pool."

The young woman eyed me suspiciously.

"I've been sent by Head Office to bring your shows back online."

"Oh, yeah, Clive said someone was coming…"

Her enthusiasm was overwhelming.

"Well, first off, I need the logbooks so I can see how far the dolphins have progressed. Then I'll need plenty of cut fish so I can start training."

She clearly didn't like taking orders from a total stranger and ungraciously dumped the journals on the kitchen table.

They didn't make inspiring reading.

The show – if you could call it that – had fully collapsed at least a month back, so no wonder Rothwell had needed me so urgently. Even more troubling, half the workforce weren't even proper presenters, just casual fairground fodder drafted in from the amusement park. None of them had a clue what they were doing, proving yet again that West Coast badly needed the expertise of a trainer.

For the rest of that day, I worked dolphins who appeared to be emotionally starved and desperate for human contact – a fact I found incredibly disturbing. So, after completing the final training session, I made it my business to complain about their treatment to the elusive Clive Rothwell. After some effort, I eventually found him entombed within a poky office at the entrance to Fun City.

Our unscheduled meeting started out tensely, but within minutes grew relaxed and friendly. Clive gave the impression of being a decent, hard-working bloke who'd been left to struggle alone and unsupported by the Company hierarchy.

He explained how Backhouse had been instrumental in revising staff policy, deeming trainers to be a costly luxury whilst assuring his area managers that, "Anyone with a whistle and a fish bucket can train a dolphin."

Familiar words from a man whose envy of trainers was becoming ever more apparent, confirming what I most feared: Backhouse had indeed become the driving force behind Company strategy, strengthening his own position by covertly manipulating policy. He reminded me of a chameleon – a master of disguise. No matter how friendly this seducer might appear to be, he nursed a sinister agenda: eliminate the competition and climb the corporate ladder.

After a further three days at West Coast, I managed to bring Gerry's legacy back up to scratch, proving that all these sad and neglected dolphins needed was a little tender loving care – something the workers here seemed incapable of delivering. I was guiltily aware that they needed more of my time, but had to leave, nonetheless. I couldn't risk my beloved Hendle falling back into the clutches of Clyde.

However, I knew that my visit to West Coast had only delayed the inevitable. Its show would undoubtedly crash again and, no matter how nice a bloke Clive might seem, he'd always be led by Backhouse: a man averse to differentiating between a trainer and a presenter – a failing that would eventually return to haunt us all.

Although not even I could have foreseen the tragic impact this wretched pool would have on the fate of me and my dolphins.

❮ 36 ❯

As I stepped into the Hendle kitchen, I was mobbed by a band of relieved presenters. In just three days, Clyde had managed to send our new recruits paranoid. So, no surprise there, then!

But what was a surprise was Carol: instead of her usual indifferent nod, she greeted me by flinging her arms around my neck and telling me how much she'd missed me. Incredible! I was totally speechless – gobsmacked, in fact. I'd always been under the impression that she didn't like me, which just showed how little I knew about girls. There was no doubt that my ice maiden was melting... and melting fast!

When I finally managed to escape Carol's prolonged bear-hug, my first task was to report back to Backhouse, informing him of the dire situation at West Coast – albeit taking care not to mention my friendly chat with Clive Rothwell.

"Look, Tommy, West Coast is a disaster waiting to happen. You've got to get a trainer in there, or at least someone who has a vague idea what they're doing."

Backhouse again opened his mouth rather than his ears. "West Coast has plenty of staff and doesn't need any more."

"But Tommy..."

He held up a hand. "It's not up for discussion. You've done what was asked and it no longer concerns you."

I was seething. "Okay, well let's talk about something that *does* concern me – Hendle. I notice that all my dolphins have started shedding skin again, which means the water's turning. High season's not far off and, if they get sick due to the water, they won't be able to perform. And, if that happens, not only will the men in suits lose a fortune, but Head Office will hold you personally responsible."

He listened thoughtfully before informing me that he would monitor the situation and "make a decision in due time". Clearly, the thought of losing the bank holiday bonanza for Rogers and Co had struck home.

So, my last four days had been most productive. Firstly, I'd made peace with the West Coast manager; secondly, I'd finally persuaded Backhouse to take the water situation seriously; and, just to top it off, it looked as if I might have found myself a girlfriend.

Great! Now, it's been a long time – so what do I do with a girlfriend?

<h1 style="text-align:center">❧ 37 ❧</h1>

Over the next few weeks, the persistent Carol stalked me relentlessly, tirelessly shadowing my every move. There was no mistaking her dogged determination as she zeroed in on her hapless quarry… me!

Although flattering, the entire situation unnerved me, as I was still very naïve in the ways of girls. However, outgunned and outmanoeuvred, I finally capitulated to her advances. Thus, my fate was sealed – I now officially had a girlfriend, eager to show me that there was indeed life beyond the walls of the dolphinarium.

In the meantime, a relatively blissful three weeks passed before I received the news I'd been longing to hear: Welby Park would definitely be open within the next four weeks, meaning I'd at last see the back of Bonnie and Clyde.

Welby Park's first show was to be a sparkling affair, attended by the Company's high rollers and a string of celebrities. But, even more thrilling and surprising, Head Office had chosen *me* to host.

I felt hugely privileged that the Company had favoured me over a recognised compère, and had to smile as I recalled those early days at Hendle when Gerry had had to trick me into picking up the microphone. How things had changed – this commission demonstrated just how talented a showman I'd become… mainly thanks to covering for Clyde's antics.

This was great news for Hendle as the gangster duo's departure would not only relieve the pressure on our overworked filters, but also signal the long-awaited start of my forward somersault training. Equally, it would free up a holding pen, enabling me to perform a full water dump if required – something Backhouse would *have to* authorise if he wanted to protect the lucrative peak season bonanza.

But the good news didn't end there: Head Office had asked Backhouse to go to Welby to supervise the new pool's completion, checking safety features, public facilities and – most importantly – water quality. In essence, this meant that I'd be getting rid of him for a full month… and, even better, he'd be gone within the week. I could hardly believe it – a glorious month of freedom to look forward to. It was a dream come true as, with him out of the way, I could carry out a partial ditch of the pool without him even knowing, meaning I wouldn't have to grovel for permission.

So, good times ahead. In less than fifteen days, Bonnie and Clyde would be following Backhouse to Welby and I'd be pulling the plug on the Hendle pool.

And about time, too!

As expected, Backhouse conveniently left for Welby without giving consent for a partial pool dump, saying he'd reconsider on his return. In other words, he was playing for time – as usual.

So, no surprise there. Deep down, I'd always known that he'd put Company profits before the welfare of my dolphins. Nevertheless, I was acutely aware that, by the time he did return, we'd be well on our way to high season, making a ditch impossible due to contractual agreements with the safari park's owners – meaning it was once again down to me.

Any further delay would pose a significant threat to the health of my dolphins, so as soon as Backhouse was on his way, I summoned all new recruits to the filter room – risky, because I couldn't rely on them not to tell tales. However, the water situation was now so dire, I had to throw caution to the wind.

"Listen up, people, I don't have to tell you how bad the water is – you already know. Not only does the pool stink, but also our dolphins are peeling and swimming around with their eyes closed. In other words, they're burning up in their own waste – and using extra chlorine isn't gonna make things any better. Now, does anybody *not* understand what I've just said?"

No reply – only concerned faces.

"You're also aware of a certain Company policy that prohibits water dumping without direct consent from vets and Management – a policy our general manager values above all else."

More uneasy looks.

"I cannot and will not allow my dolphins to suffer any longer – they've suffered long enough. So tonight, I intend to carry out a partial pool dump – something I can't do alone. I need at least one volunteer to work the filters. All I ask from the rest of you is that you keep your mouths shut and say nothing – especially not to Backhouse."

Rebellious debate animated the filter room, quickly generating my first dissident. A few minutes more and all had joined our ranks.

"Right, people, let's get this done! We're in for a long night. For starters, I need at least thirty bags of salt stacking on the poolside…"

Once the backwash had started, we had nothing more to do but sit around and watch the pool's toxic mix disappearing down the drains – truly a welcome sight. However, this partial ditch would only ever be a stopgap, as any bad water remaining was bound to contaminate the fresh.

Still, as they used to say in the Shire, "Owt's better than nowt!"

❦ 39 ❧

Two glorious Backhouse-free weeks later, the day I'd been dreaming of finally arrived: Bonnie and Clyde's transport to Welby Park.

With these two, a regular pool catch would be nigh impossible – they were fully mature dolphins who wouldn't surrender their freedom lightly. A competent catcher I might be, but I had no intention of going head-to-head with either one of them in open water... particularly not Clyde. So, before Philip's arrival, I chose the easier option of gating them into the confines of a pen.

It was certainly good to see Philip again as, for the last twelve months, the playboy vet had been plying his trade in the lucrative European and Middle Eastern markets, meaning I'd been dealing instead with his junior assistant, Tony Forrester. I'd particularly missed the vet's friendly banter, and we spent several minutes catching up before starting the transport proper.

For Dan, this was his first official catch, so he was understandably nervous and needed a few words of encouragement.

"If you don't think, Dan, you won't get hurt. Understand?"

He nodded breathlessly. "Yeah... I understand... don't think... don't think... don't think..."

First up was Bonnie, our gentle giant, who drifted accommodatingly into her harness, almost as if she were going on a picnic.

"There, that wasn't so bad, was it?"

Dan's face was awash with relief.

"Now for the easy one... Clyde..."

"Don't think… don't think… don't think… don't think…"

Clyde, of course, was more aggressive, wriggling and twisting in an attempt to bite my legs. But, in the end, even he was defeated by his cramped conditions and within forty minutes, both he and Bonnie were safely ensconced in the back of the transport, along with all those presenters destined for Welby.

Bidding a quick farewell to Dan and Carol, I took my place beside them, and it wasn't long before we were speeding through Hendle's main gates en route to the new Welby Park dolphinarium.

"No more Bonnie and Clyde, it's like a dream come true," I announced joyously. "Fantastic!"

I was finding it hard to contain my enthusiasm. Not only was I getting rid of these two disruptive dolphins, but in just seven days' time, I would be hosting the most prestigious event in the country. In just one week, *I* would be entertaining celebrity. It didn't come any bigger than that…

… who would have believed it?

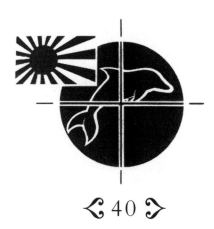

❦ 40 ❧

On our arrival at Welby, I was surprised to find the usual media circus absent. Instead, we were greeted by gangs of construction workers who milled around the dolphinarium like angry ants – a sure sign that the pool was behind schedule.

As I walked inside, the first thing to hit me was the condition of the water: dull and cloudy, it swallowed sunlight and reeked of chemicals. Appalled, I scanned my surroundings. "Where's Tommy?"

Suddenly, a flustered and white-faced Backhouse emerged from the filter room. "Things haven't gone to plan – I've had problems with the water," he moaned.

It seemed that, in an effort to impress, he'd tried to manage the water himself, assuring Rogers and the Board that they needn't waste money on a costly filtration expert. And, stupidly, they'd chosen to believe him.

"What about Bonnie and Clyde?" I snapped. "They're harnessed and waiting in the back of the van, and I can't put them in *that*…"

"Oh, they'll be all right," he replied. "We'll sort the water out later."

I couldn't believe what I was hearing. "Sort the water out later? What kind of answer is that? There's no way I can put Bonnie and Clyde in there."

Backhouse glanced around uncomfortably, checking for unwelcome ears. "Look, don't argue, just do as you're told. I don't want every Tom, Dick and Harry knowing our business."

Once again, his overriding desire to save money and impress Head Office had won the day, leaving me, as always, to pick up the pieces.

I was fuming, absolutely fuming!

True, I was no fan of Clyde and couldn't wait to get rid of him and his partner – but not like this… *never* like this. Backhouse had been at Welby for well over two weeks supposedly sorting things out, yet – once again – he'd failed to deliver. So what the heck *had* he been doing?

Struggling to speak calmly, I repeated my objections. "You can't expect me to dump Bonnie and Clyde in this – it'll make them ill."

Typically, the agitated Backhouse refused to reply, retreating instead into the safety of the filter room. I stood alone on the stage, dazedly wondering what to do next. I didn't have the authority to take Bonnie and Clyde back to Hendle, but nor could I leave them in the van to catch cold. I had no alternative but to follow Backhouse's orders and release them into the murky waters.

Once the commotion surrounding their transfer had died down, I anxiously checked the water readings. Not good: unnaturally high chlorine levels and low salt. Something had to be done… and done quickly.

Galvanizing my team into action, we attempted to redress the salt/fresh water balance by emptying large bags of salt into the pool – although, frustratingly, there was nothing we could do about the high chlorine levels, because Backhouse had forgotten to order the all-important hypo crystals necessary for chlorine neutralization.

We worked solidly for the rest of the day, striving to make things at least bearable for Bonnie and Clyde. And, throughout it all, Backhouse was conspicuous by his absence – a situation that suited me down to the ground. Events at Hendle had already put our relationship under an intolerable strain…

… but, after this débâcle, I could hardly bear to even look at him.

❦ 41 ❦

Incredibly, the dolphinarium was ready on time for its première show – despite the cloudy water and scent of chemicals in the air. Clearly, the new filters were still bedding-down – something a qualified water engineer would have allowed for.

Without the required hypo crystals, the pool was still awash with stinging chlorine, forcing Bonnie and Clyde to swim with their eyes tight shut. Under these conditions, I knew they'd be hard-pressed to complete the opening day's four allotted shows, so, for me, it was all about muddling through. Thankfully, tomorrow I'd be out of here and on my way back home to Hendle – a luxury denied these two unfortunate dolphins.

The atmosphere between Backhouse and me was so tense that we'd barely exchanged a word since my arrival. However, one of the few things he did share with me was his intention to remain at Welby for at least another fortnight to iron out any teething problems. Well, he could expect to be busy, because, as sure as day was day, Bonnie and Clyde would pack in work, leaving no one with any experience to bring them back online.

All in all, my dream show had suddenly deteriorated into a smash and grab operation – in and out with the greatest possible speed. Nevertheless, I endeavoured to banish my concerns and concentrate on the upcoming performance. Despite all the problems, this was still the biggest show I'd ever been involved in, so I had to get it right – and Management delivering last minute script changes to my opening spiel didn't make things any easier.

Everyone was a bag of nerves – none more so than the jittery Backhouse.

"David, the nation's press will be out there today, so there can't be any mistakes – the show's got to go right."

I detected an almost pleading note in his voice. My general manager was definitely feeling the pressure.

"Look, Tommy, I can only do my best, but, for what it's worth, I think we'll get away with the opening show. But as for the other three… well, they're in the lap of the gods."

Realising the implications of what I'd said, he shrieked with horror. "But it's our opening day! All the top people will be here… we can't cancel shows today… we just can't!"

I was actually beginning to feel sorry for him. "It's not down to me, Tommy – it's down to Bonnie and Clyde. You know the state the water's in. You'll just have to pray that they're able to cope."

With a final, agitated look, he turned, then scurried out of the kitchen, shaking his head and muttering, "But we can't cancel shows… we just can't!"

There was little point in indulging in the blame game. It wasn't necessary – he already knew who was responsible.

❦ 42 ❧

Dumping my filthy work gear, I showered and dressed in preparation for Welby's première show. By this time, conditions in the staff room resembled a free for all – a hustle and bustle of people frantically tearing off clothing and hogging mirrors. We were all literally fighting to look our best – a philosophy not lost on the Company, which had supplied us with brand-new designer uniforms: red miniskirts and white tops for the girls, and extra-flared trousers and tight-fitting red tee shirts for the boys. We were all very much dressed to impress.

I felt like a giant Barbie doll as those girls not involved in the show-proper delighted in applying my stage make-up and setting my hair. And, though I say so myself, by the time they'd finished, I didn't look half bad. Giving myself a final once-over in the mirror, I proudly announced before all and sundry, "You good-looking thing, Capello! Now get out there and knock 'em dead!"

Peeking around the stage door, I saw that the auditorium was largely empty. The fifty or so people seated – VIPs and members of the press – had been handpicked for the event, reaffirming that this was the hottest ticket in town. As the background music faded into silence, I walked confidently onto the stage – only to be confronted by poker-faced dignitaries.

The experience was surreal, almost intimidating, as we performed to virtually no applause, the hierarchies watching dispassionately as though attending a Command Performance…

… "Entertain me!"

I'd always known that this show would be different, but never expected this. Nevertheless, we soldiered on, and Bonnie and Clyde – to their credit – performed to the best of their abilities considering the adverse water conditions.

Once the show had ended, the men in suits performed their usual celebratory ritual of backslapping and photo-calls before scurrying off to enjoy their customary freebies. As the last of the guests disappeared for lunch, Rogers made his way down to the stage area to offer his congratulations.

"Wonderful job, David! Your show commentary was superb, even if a little risqué in places." He coughed drolly, then beamed a satisfied smile.

I responded with a cheeky smirk. He was right, of course – I had strayed into risqué waters, especially bold considering our esteemed guests. "A bit of sass always wakes them up," I laughed.

Backhouse stood by his side, smiling, but still plainly agitated. "Well, Mr Rogers, we're on a tight schedule today, so let's not keep our guests waiting…" And with that remark, he rudely cut short our conversation, before bustling Rogers to the exit, thus ensuring that I didn't get chance to comment on the water.

So far, the tormented Bonnie and Clyde had worked like Trojans, their sheer professionalism carrying them through. But I didn't expect their commitment to stretch through another three shows – a fear borne out during their next performance, when we just about got by.

Not so the third show, however, which totally collapsed as Bonnie and Clyde downed tools and left the stage, leaving me to talk my way through a performance that produced nothing – not one single trick.

A glum-faced Backhouse – returned early from the corporate festivities – watched from the auditorium as his worst fears were realised. After the disappointed audience had gone, he descended to the stage, where he dithered despondently.

"Tommy," I snapped, "I'm not putting up with another show like this. Just get me off this bloody stage!"

"Please, David, you know how important today is. We can't cancel any shows… we can't!"

I was in no mood for arguing. "Well, tell that to Bonnie and Clyde, because I'm through covering. If you want more shows, you can do them yourself. I mean it, Tommy... I'm gone!"

Begrudgingly and dispiritedly, he finally complied by cancelling the last show. Meanwhile, news filtered through that a jubilant Management – drunk with success over its newest venture and still ignorant of the water conditions – had issued invitations to a celebratory meal. My heart plummeted. More hassle – these thank you functions always made me feel like a spare part.

After changing, I returned to the pool room – the heavy smell of chemicals still choking the air – to bid a final farewell to a clearly distressed Bonnie and Clyde. Bonnie, as always, came into the stage for a cuddle, but a disgruntled Clyde kept his distance and showed his displeasure by angrily smashing his tail on the water's surface.

"I'm really sorry, Bonnie. I'm leaving you in a right mess, aren't I, girl?"

She lifted her head, eyes glued shut – yet another sobering reminder of Backhouse's gross incompetence. Even more distressing, I was powerless to help as the promised hypo crystals had still not materialised – yet another glorious Backhouse oversight.

A final tickle under Bonnie's chin signalled an end to my involvement with this gangster duo. I'd never see them again. But, as I prepared to close the door behind me, I couldn't resist one last backward glance: Bonnie and Clyde swimming into my past, endowing me with the shameful memory of two distraught dolphins weaving chlorine-clouded water.

And to think I'd actually felt sorry for Backhouse... my mistake.

❦ 43 ❦

Within the hour, I had joined an animated batch of Welby presenters, eager to sample the delights of their first celebratory bash.

The guest list included Ken Rogers, our ever-popular vet, Philip, and, of course, Backhouse. In fact, the only notable absentee from the line-up was my friend and former boss, Will Chadderton – now the official manager of Welby, but sidelined on a month's sick leave. More's the pity – especially for Bonnie and Clyde – because the water problems would never have arisen had he been present.

As always, the lavish affair started rather sedately with everyone on their best behaviour. However, as the night progressed and the drinks started flowing – fuelled by a free Company bar – people began to let themselves go.

The consumption of large amounts of alcohol continued joyously under the watchful eyes of Rogers and his now permanent shadow, Backhouse.

It was during this celebratory binge that I noticed one of the new girl presenters wobbling in their direction. Giddily eager to impress her new bosses, she animatedly began to outline her ideas on how to improve the show. Both Philip and I watched tensely as the tipsy young girl proceeded to dig herself into an ever-deeper hole. Covering my mouth, I whispered to Philip, "She should watch her step, because she's definitely out of her league with those two."

Philip said nothing, but nodded soberly.

Sensing blood, Backhouse continued to egg her on, skilfully herding her like a lamb to the slaughter. But when the normally placid Rogers unexpectedly joined him, the spiteful dissection climbed to a whole new level and, within moments, both men were delighting in verbally savaging her, eviscerating her like a pair of hungry hyenas.

Mortified, I looked to Philip in silent appeal, but he evaded my gaze, embarrassment palpable as he kept his eyes fixed firmly on the table.

I didn't stay for long after that, but used my long drive back to Hendle as an excuse to leave. Truth was, however, I couldn't bear to be in Backhouse's or Rogers' company any longer. I found them both detestable.

As for the naïve teenager, for her the party was over – along with her career and all her dreams of celebrity…

… forever lost in a glass of cheap plonk.

❧ 44 ❧

Sickened to the stomach by the behaviour of my so-called superiors, I disconsolately escaped the party. I'd known Rogers for well over two years and, although undoubtedly firm, he'd always been fair… and never, never nasty. Yet, here he was, corrupted into behaving like a twisted schoolboy bully by the manipulative Backhouse.

Their disgraceful exhibition made me realise that there was little point in deluding myself any longer. It was obvious that Rogers had been suckered into putting total trust in this new messiah of the dolphin project. He had been seduced into bestowing immense power on a man who'd never actually trained a dolphin – an unbelievably naïve decision that would one day cost us all dearly.

To all intents and purposes, a jackal now sat in the President's chair.

As for me, yet again sickened by this world of people, I craved a return to the dolphin realm I loved.

Besides, Backhouse had cost me enough time – I had a forward somersault to train.

❧ 45 ❧

On arriving at Hendle, I was greeted by an excited Dan and Carol. "Happy to see me?" I groaned, "because I'm certainly happy to see you... Welby's been a nightmare!"

Predictably, Carol was first to the draw. "Nightmare? What do you mean, nightmare? We've been stuck here slaving away while you've been off enjoying yourself." Tossing back her long black hair, she laughed. "Anyway, how did the grand opening go? And, more importantly, where's our esteemed general manager? I'm surprised he's not with you."

I took a deep breath of good old northern air before answering. "Don't go there... don't even mention his name. The very thought of that man gives me a nasty rash! Anyway, how have things been here?"

Snatching the words from Carol's mouth, Dan dived in. "Well, Baby and Scouse are great. In fact, they're more than great – they've been carrying all the shows, because once you'd gone, Duchess and Herb'e point blankly refused to work."

I couldn't help smiling – my ever dependable *Perfect Pair*. No surprise. Everyone knew that, without me, my dream team wouldn't work for long. As always, it seemed they'd missed me as much as I'd missed them.

Desperate to see them again, I dashed to the poolside, dropping to my knees and flinging out my arms.

"Hello, my beautiful, beautiful people... have you missed me?"

My non-verbal greeting catapulted through the ether, bringing all four dolphins racing to the stage – excited messages and dolphin laughter knitted into a kaleidoscope of chatter that bounced like a ping-pong ball around my head. A wonderful, wonderful, chaotic reunion, all encapsulated within one extraordinary psychic bubble.

Duchess, ever shy, hung back politely, viewing me with soft eyes as I cuddled her three raucous companions – Herb'e, as always, battling for top spot.

"Yes, yes… I'm glad to see you, too…"

It had been a long time since I'd experienced such fuss from them – a sobering reminder of just how much quality time we'd lost thanks to Clyde. Then, two delightful minutes later, my three jubilant dolphins gave way, allowing me to flash my ring at Duchess.

Its enchanted call immediately drew her to the stage, where she proceeded to roll onto her back for a tickle.

"My beautiful, beautiful girl… I could eat you!"

She reciprocated by gently taking my hand into her mouth, her velvet touch imparting a sense of deep love – a magical hello before getting back down to business.

Now firmly back in my comfort zone, I had no time to dilly-dally, so excitedly began making plans for the training of the trick I coveted most – the forward somersault. For the first time in what seemed like an age, I had a pool without distractions. Bonnie and Clyde were gone and never coming back…

… just a pity the same couldn't be said about Backhouse.

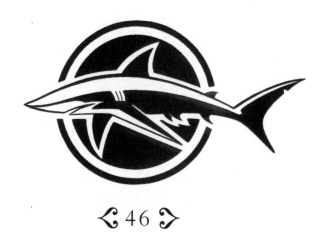

⋐ 46 ⋑

Pad and pen in hand, I called Carol and Dan into the kitchen to explain my ideas for completion of the shadow ballet. "Right, you two, sit yourselves down and let me tell you just how I mean to train this trick." Smiling widely, I delivered a corny TV adage. "Are you sitting comfortably? Then, let us begin. This is the theory: I intend to start with two ten-foot poles. The first will act as a hurdle. The second will have two beach balls attached – one at the end and the other in the centre. These balls will act as targets.

"The initial training will need two people: one to hold the hurdle-pole and another to hold the ball-pole approximately seven feet in front of it." I drew a quick sketch. "My vision is to get Duchess and Herb'e jumping over the hurdle and butting the balls before re-entering the water."

Another quick sketch. "Once they're comfortable with this, I'll raise the hurdle-pole and lower the ball-pole. This should encourage them to tipple forward into the beginnings of a half-somersault. Clear?"

Dan and Carol nodded.

"Now for the hard bit," I said, scribbling busily. "The third phase will entail whipping away the ball-pole just as Duchess and Herb'e are about to hit it, at the same time jerking the hurdle-pole up beneath their tails, effectively tipping them into a full half-forward somersault. Now, I know this sounds complicated but – believe me – it's not. It's all about timing, so we've got to get this right."

Carol and Dan again nodded.

"Once Duchess and Herb'e have achieved this, I'll introduce a hand signal so we can get rid of the heavy props." I put down my pen. "So, what do you think?"

"Have you actually seen this done?" Carol asked, frowning.

"Only in my mind, Carol, only in my mind. But once crystallized there, it won't be long before Duchess and Herb'e pick up the vision. From then on, the rest of the training will be down to me."

Again, achieving this trick would be like building a wall, brick by brick: firstly, the half-somersault would grow into a full somersault; then, the full somersault would develop into a double somersault; and so on. This was going to take some considerable time because Duchess and Herb'e would find all that jumping physically demanding. But I planned to limit each training session to only thirty minutes so as not to exhaust them.

However, whilst all this was going on, I didn't want Baby and Scouse neglecting, so decided to start them on the beaching – the trick that Bonnie and Clyde had so spectacularly made their own and a trick I'd long admired. Even better, as the beaching wasn't on Duchess and Herb'e's trick list, this would give Baby and Scouse their own little exclusive.

So thrilling times ahead for dolphins and humans alike!

I now sensed that my dream was coming to fruition. If I could successfully train the forward somersault, Duchess and Herb'e would hold the full shadow ballet – something never before seen… something that would win them worldwide recognition.

Then – and only then – would they be universally accepted as *The Perfect Pair*.

❨ 47 ❩

It had been a full month since my return from Welby Park and, thankfully, Backhouse had still not materialised. I'd heard reports that Bonnie and Clyde were performing less than half their trick list – if they performed at all – a situation that would make it increasingly difficult for him to leave.

I must admit, I found it hard to supress my delight at the notion of a rampaging Clyde raining down chaos at Welby. It conjured visions of Backhouse tearing around like a headless chicken in a desperate attempt to appease Head Office.

Mayhem, total and utterly delightful mayhem… great!

Even better, Welby's troubles would keep Hendle a Backhouse-free zone for even longer, meaning great news all round!

Good old Clyde – about time he did me a favour!

❦ 48 ❧

Disturbing news: I'd heard whispers that the West Coast show had again collapsed. Not surprising, but worrying, particularly as *I* now seemed to be the Company's trouble-shooter of choice, meaning that any problems arising there would impact directly on me – and this seaside dolphinarium had already stolen enough of my time.

On a happier note, Hendle's was now the only show running smoothly, both my dolphin teams performing diligently in joyful expectation of their evening training sessions.

It was good to have a happy pool again.

The amazing Baby and Scouse were still progressing at a fantastic rate. Scouse particularly loved the beaching trick; but, unfortunately, the same couldn't be said about his infant partner, who adamantly refused to leave the water. However, I no longer viewed this as a problem – these dolphins were clearly individuals, so I simply dropped Baby from the trick and allowed Scouse a solo... after all, there could only ever be one *Perfect Pair*.

Speaking of Duchess and Herb'e, the forward somersault was still progressing very slowly with both dolphins apparently struggling to understand exactly what was needed. Despite five weeks of relentless training, we'd made only limited headway. Still, they both seemed happy, which was no surprise because, since the start of training, their fish consumption had virtually doubled. They were piling on the pounds – especially around the bellies – meaning I had two excessively contented and podgy dolphins!

As with most nights, somersault training attracted helpers – Carol, Dan and the ever-eager young Graham – always appreciated as the heavy training poles played havoc with my arm muscles. Still, if any trick was worth the sacrifice, it was this one.

It was during this period of relative calm that I decided to ask for a pay rise. I still hadn't received any recompense for being the Company's sole trainer, yet my two dolphin pairs were now considered star entertainers, drawing Joe Public from far and wide. There was no doubt that my four dolphins were reaping rich rewards for the Company, so with Hendle's show on an all-time high, I decided to press my advantage by submitting a formal request on Backhouse's return. Even though we didn't get on, I couldn't see him refusing...

... after all, after what I'd achieved, how could he?

❦ 49 ❧

When Backhouse eventually returned, I immediately asked him to submit my request for a pay rise to Head Office – only to have him refuse.

"A new policy has been introduced, which means the Company will no longer be granting any individual pay increases." He shot me a condescending look. "All presenter pay is now standardised – and there will be no exceptions."

I couldn't believe what I was hearing. Thanks to me, Hendle had the two finest dolphin teams in the country – a fact he was conveniently choosing to ignore. But what I found even more insulting, even more galling, was his reference to my new job title.

"So, I'm classed as a presenter now, am I?" I growled.

A prolonged silence gave me his answer.

Soul destroying – my reward for all that hard slog was to be demoted to the lesser rank of everyday presenter.

It was blatantly obvious that Backhouse harboured an obsessive jealousy of trainers – a jealousy that bordered on hatred – no doubt exacerbated by the recent indignities inflicted upon him by Clyde at Welby. Even so, it must have taken some gargantuan effort on his part to finally sway a gullible Head Office into believing that it no longer needed trainers at all…

… I was stunned.

Then, to add insult to injury, he casually announced, "I want you to drive up to West Coast today. The show has collapsed and Clive Rothwell needs you to put it right."

Needs *me* to put it right…? Unbelievable!

"Are you joking, or what? If my skills are so commonplace, why does Clive need *me*?" I shook my head in exasperation. "No… no way… I'm not going. As you keep reminding everybody, 'anyone with a whistle and a fish bucket can train a dolphin', so get one of your other *presenters* to do it, because this one is refusing. Or, better still, do it yourself!" I stormed out of his office, giving him no time to formulate a reply.

But little did I realise that this refusal would one day trigger a managerial decision that would prove catastrophic for both me and my dolphins.

There was no going back – the die had been cast.

❧ 50 ❧

My refusal to fly to West Coast's rescue gave Backhouse yet another excuse to withhold permission for a full pool dump, although, thankfully, he remained unaware of the partial ditch I'd carried out during his absence. Nevertheless, despite that stealthy act of disobedience, my calculations told me that the water would be turning toxic by August – a circumstance I was quick to press home.

As usual, he took my warning with the proverbial pinch of salt. It seemed that my power-mad general manager was even prepared to risk losing the biggest crowds of the year just to prove that he was boss.

As the season got into full swing, six or seven shows a day and two nightly training sessions mercifully kept him off my back. In the meantime, I watched with growing concern as the water deteriorated even faster than I'd predicted.

A further anxiety at this time was the progress of the forward somersault... or, should I say, lack of it. We were getting nowhere fast. Up to press, all I'd managed to do was get Duchess and Herb'e jumping the hurdle to hit the balls – I just couldn't get them to tip into the somersault. For some reason, our normally ice-clear *connection* had become fuzzy and confused, as if lacking the necessary fine-tuning – something I'd been aware of for some time.

Initially, I chose to blame this on my bruising encounters with Clyde but, without doubt, the situation with Backhouse wasn't helping, either. I was becoming constantly on edge and dangerously hyper – signs that I may well be falling ill again.

Yet it wasn't just the feud with Backhouse. Something else was rocking the boat... something I couldn't quite put my finger on...

It wasn't Herb'e. He was positively bouncing as he made the most of his fish bonanza – having a ball as he continued to pile on the pounds, developing at least three double chins in the process.

No, it definitely wasn't old fat-face...

... it was Duchess... Duchess was the problem.

She seemed far away and unable to concentrate, straining our close psychic link. I also noticed that, when coming into the stage, instead of looking at me, she seemed to be scanning the area behind me, as if something or someone were distracting her.

This was puzzling as the only activity there was when a member of staff occasionally walked from the kitchen to the filter room – something that had never bothered her before. So why was it bothering her now?

"What's wrong, beautiful, don't you love me anymore?"

I'd just asked the wrong question. Swinging her head around sharply, Duchess glared at me before crashing her tail on the water and swimming away.

"What's up with her?" Dan commented. "She's got a right cob on!"

"Not a clue," I replied bewilderedly, "not a clue."

I watched with concern as she purposely avoided the stage area, choosing instead to meander at the furthest corner of the pool – as far away from me as possible. She was going to great lengths to show me her displeasure.

"Okay, Duchess, if that's the way you want it, stay there! I've got better things to do than hang around here all night trying to placate you."

A smirking Dan watched from the auditorium. "Man, you *are* in her bad books. I've never seen her like this with you before."

I shook my head. "Women – what can you do with them?"

And just to plunge the dagger a little deeper, a squawk of delight radiated from a triple-chinned Herb'e who was clearly enjoying my chastisement.

"I don't know what you're laughing at, Herb'e, but you obviously know something I don't..."

His generous mouth opened even wider and I felt the fuse of static rushing behind my eyes. Crafty Claude had just beamed me a message – one I didn't understand. And, what's more, he knew it.

"Enjoy it while you can, Herb'e... you comedian!"

I turned to Dan. "Look, Carol's already legged it and I'm not prepared to waste any more time here, so let's get an early dip and go."

I fed the remaining fish to Baby and Scouse, then changed for my nightly swim. Adjusting my facemask, I quietly slipped into the water's cool embrace. The ripples in the mirror barely had time to dissipate before Duchess' sleek form weaved across its plane, gently and purposefully hemming me in before rolling over to expose a soft underbelly.

"That's more like it. Have you forgiven me, beautiful?"

Feeling cocooned in a shawl of love, I suddenly became aware that she was using her body to paint patterns onto the liquid canvas – a watery brushwork that encircled me with silky caresses. It was amazing, as if the currents she generated had a life of their own.

Then, abruptly, her masterpiece was spoiled as a boisterous Herb'e, determined not to be left out, bulldozed between us to thrust his bulky head onto my shoulders.

"What's going on here? Am I missing something?"

"Take it easy, lad – we're not going anywhere."

Hustling me into a close-quarter wrestle, he playfully pushed Duchess aside...

Big mistake!

Duchess' response was immediate: her mood changed dramatically, shocking us both to attention, raw emotion snapping through our psyches as she mentally and physically barged a bemused Herb'e out of the way.

"Get lost, Herb'e – leave us alone!"

The expression in her eyes was dark, even menacing.

"I mean it, Herb'e... stay out of our way!"

I might not be fully tuned-in to the dolphin radio, but even I couldn't mistake Duchess' psychic threat. My Atlantean princess meant business.

A shocked Herb'e meandered uncertainly before sheepishly giving way to the demands of our new *domina*, choosing instead to resume his sub-aqua meanderings in the more amenable company of Baby and Scouse.

"Gosh, you're in a funny mood, aren't you, Duch?" I said, gently cupping her snout.

At my touch, her anger seemed to wash away; then, with all distractions gone, she resumed in her girlish play, pushing first into my right side, then into my left, before reopening a velvet-soft *connection*.

"Just what is wrong with you?"

Still ignoring the other dolphins, she turned on her side, gently but firmly grabbing my hand in her mouth, then proceeded to lead me to her newly-adopted corner of the pool. It was obvious that tonight she didn't intend to share me with anyone.

After the swim, it struck me as strange how none of the other dolphins had attempted to approach us – except for Herb'e, of course, just before Duchess had barged him away. It was as if they were honouring an ancient charter and to break it would be 'crossing the line'.

The whole experience had felt surreal.

This hadn't been that special *connection* we'd always shared, but something else – something entirely different…

… almost intimidating.

❦ 51 ❧

I was still perplexed after the previous night's playtime swim with Duchess, her aggressive mood swings playing on my mind – alien behaviour, which would hopefully dissipate during the hurly-burly of today's shows.

Thank goodness for the reliability of Baby and Scouse, whose performances continued to go from strength to strength. Amazing when I thought back to the day they'd first arrived: a frightened infant and a blinded dolphin, branded as two throwaways surplus to requirements. How things had changed! My miniature duo was now one of the country's top performing teams.

"You're my two little superstars, aren't you?"

As always, my eager beavers couldn't wait to get going. Their enthusiasm was boundless. They never seemed to have an off day and constantly revelled in new challenges – unlike their more esteemed counterparts, Duchess and Herb'e, who were constantly throwing tantrums.

Baby and Scouse literally wore their hearts on their flippers, fervently displaying their appreciation at finding a place where they belonged. Their love of Hendle – and each other – was clear for all to see, and our close association left me feeling immensely fulfilled.

After the first three shows, I gated my two little stars and introduced Duchess and Herb'e into the main pool. Both seemed excited as they surveyed the crowd from behind the security railings. But, once the show was underway, Duchess began to intimidate Herb'e, forcing him from the stage – a complete role reversal from those first days at Hendle.

"Come on, Duchess, what's wrong with you? Let Herb'e come in to the stage! You know I won't allow you to work alone."

Disappointingly, as the day wore on, Duchess' behaviour towards her partner became increasingly aggressive… yet, strangely, ever more gentle towards me. Even so, she was missing her usual girlish *connection*. Her radio was on, but her transmission was wild and chaotic, a frenzied mishmash of raw emotion that flashed and danced behind my eyes.

More proof that something else was going on… something completely different from anything I'd experienced before.

"What is it, Duch? What do you want?"

No answer – just a sweet smelling nausea drinking my troubles away. As she fixed me with her gaze, I once again found myself falling into those vivid blue eyes.

"My beautiful, beautiful Duchess…"

❦ 52 ❧

"Dan," I sighed, "after the day I've had with Duchess, I'm totally out of the game! Let's give the playtime swim a miss and have an early night."

There were only Dan and I left in the dolphinarium, Carol having already gone home – something that was becoming a regular occurrence.

"It's no wonder you're always tired, Dave," Dan commented. "You never stop working. You need to get away from this place and have a bit of fun."

Easier said than done – these last six months had been hard... draining, in fact.

"Why don't you take Carol out once in a while?" he suggested. "After all, you're supposed to be her boyfriend."

He was right – I was supposed to be her boyfriend. Yet more words of wisdom from my starship second officer. Maybe I needed a break to get myself together. After all, my present lifestyle was all work and no play, leaving me little time for anything other than my dolphins, and Carol had been the main casualty of my obsession. I'd been a rotten companion and, if I didn't pull my socks up, I might well lose her.

"Yeah, Dan, you're right, absolutely right," I nodded sagely. "Things are gonna change. Things are definitely gonna change. Carol and me are gonna start having a good time... start painting the town ... yeah, we are...

... just as soon as I've got the somersault, of course!"

❧ 53 ❧

All next day, I struggled to keep my two stars focussed, as a disgruntled Duchess persisted with her spoiling tactics. Completion of the final show came as a welcome relief.

"Thank God that's over!" Dan complained. "She's been like this for four days now and I'm running out of excuses." Dan was having difficulty recovering from yet another testing day on the mic.

Carol, as always, was quick to add her two-penn'orth. "Never mind four days – it's been at least a week. That's why I've been skipping my swim and leaving early... I don't trust her."

"Don't trust her?" I immediately jumped to Duchess' defence – girlfriend or not, I wouldn't allow any bad-mouthing of my precious princess. "What do you mean 'don't trust her'? There's nothing wrong with Duchess... she's okay... just going through a funny patch, that's all."

Me and my big mouth – I'd just given the wrong answer.

"Oh, there's a surprise," Carol snapped. "That's just typical of you! In your eyes, she can do no wrong... all sweetness and light... but, I'm telling you, she's not to be trusted... she's dangerous."

My fervent defence of Duchess had clearly got Carol's back up, so, in the interest of self-preservation, I decided to beat a hasty retreat. Smiling innocently, I replied, "Anyway, I'm going for a swim now. Catch you both later..."

Within seconds of my entering the mirror, Duchess' sleek form skimmed its plane.

"Hello, beautiful, happy to see me?

Even beneath the bite of my snorkel, I found it impossible not to smile as an overpowering feeling of love flooded my entire being. Moving together, we weaved through liquid sky in search of deeper water, whilst Herb'e, Baby and Scouse played their games at a respectful distance.

"Nothing wrong with you, is there, Duchess?"

Everything was going fine – until Carol appeared onstage wearing her swimsuit. Her sudden appearance sparked the vixen within – on spying her, Duchess' entire body stiffened, the soft *connection* that had enveloped me only moments earlier usurped by something dark and unforgiving.

Carol, too, sensed the change, gazing into the mirror's face, motionless and afraid.

Duchess darted towards her, stopping only inches from the poolside, sumptuous form morphing into something hunched and rigid... a shadowy shape drifting like a log in a lake.

Glancing at me anxiously, Carol took a tentative step towards the pool's edge, then dipped her toe into the watery arena.

"That's as far as you go, bitch...!"

A tsunami of rage, hatred and raw jealousy smashed over the stage, a psychic shockwave followed by a graphic physical display – frenzied head challenges and bouts of heavy tail slapping.

"You're not getting in here..."

Visibly shaken, Carol backed away to drift bewilderedly towards the far side of the stage, but a determined Duchess followed, shadowing her every move.

"Set one foot in here... just one foot...' and you've had it!"

Retreating again, Carol shouted to me across the water. "David, she won't let me in!"

That was an understatement if ever I'd heard one. "I can see that, Carol," I shouted back. "It's no good pushing it... I think you'd better give tonight's swim a miss."

Visibly relieved, she nodded, then tiptoed back to the kitchen.

No sooner had she disappeared from view than a gleeful Duchess swam back to my side to bury her head beneath my arm.

"What was all that about, Duch?"

Again, she didn't answer, but resumed her velvet swing of the previous evening, pushing me gently from side to side with her head. It felt almost as if she were dancing – a ritual ballet as old as time.

"What are you doing, Duch?"

The longer she danced, the more chaotic her song: the more chaotic her song, the rougher the dance... almost frenzied. Then, abruptly and without warning, she rolled herself over, exposing her soft white underbelly.

Like a bolt out of the blue, it hit me! What an idiot – how could I have been so blind? Duchess was conducting a courtship, choosing a mate... and she'd chosen me. Like a fool, I'd totally missed what was so glaringly obvious: the light of my life, sensing my close attachment to Carol, had been using a marked display of aggression to repel the competition...

... a threat Carol had instinctively sensed.

You stupid, stupid man, Capello...!

This sudden revelation, compounded by Duchess' continuing amorous advances, hurled me back to reality.

"Wait a minute, Duch... what about poor Herb'e?"

What about poor Herb'e...? What the hell was I saying? Bizarre – at a time like this, all I could think about was my jilted friend.

"What about him?" Duchess shrieked.

What could I say? I was obviously in well over my head, the situation far more than I could cope with, so – for the second time that day – I resorted to beating a hasty exit.

"Got to go... got to go...!"

Duchess trailed after me mournfully.

"What are you doing, David? Where are you going? Don't leave... please, don't leave!"

Still flustered, I dragged myself to the sanctuary of the poolside, leaving my dejected admirer soulfully looking on.

"Sorry, Duch, got things to do... can't stay... got lots of things to do..."

Talk about making your excuses – this one took the biscuit!

Nevertheless, the experience had left me shell-shocked – not to mention overwhelmed by a heart-breaking feeling of guilt. My poor Duchess…

Today's events had resurrected the memory of our first fateful encounter – that magical moment when a princess from Atlantis had become infatuated with a boy and his band of gold.

Duchess had chosen me then – all those years ago – and I drew little comfort from knowing that I'd shattered her dreams. I felt like a heel – the lowest of the low – as if I'd betrayed her.

But most of all, I felt sad, terribly, terribly sad as I finally realised that my little Atlantean princess… wasn't so little anymore.

❦ 54 ❧

After showering, I joined Carol and Dan in the kitchen, where we discussed Duchess' flirtatious overtures over a pot of hot tea.

"I just can't believe it!" Dan smiled, shaking his head. "It's amazing... absolutely amazing!"

Amazing it might be, but, for Carol, as a student of marine biology, the implications were far more profound. "I'd heard that dolphins were promiscuous, but I'd never dreamed of anything like this – to think that a dolphin could seriously regard a human as a prospective mate... unbelievable." She shook her head. "The more I see of dolphin behaviour, the more I feel like dumping my text books!"

"Well, how do you think I feel?" I wailed. "I've worked for years to keep Duchess and Herb'e together and now I feel like the marriage guidance counsellor who's just become the third party problem." What I didn't confess, however, was just how totally devastated I was feeling at having so hurt Duchess. Although my friends might find the notion of her impossible love amusing, to me, it was little short of heart breaking. My poor, poor princess...

"Well," Carol added archly, "I did warn you... I told you and told you that..."

Thankfully, a loud banging on the kitchen door interrupted her oncoming rebuke.

"Who the hell can this be at this time of night?" Dan asked, a note of alarm creeping into his voice.

Furtively opening the door, I peeked outside to find a wet and bedraggled security guard peering at me through the rain. He seemed agitated. "Can yer let me in, please?"

This was the last thing I needed – it had been a long day and I desperately wanted to go home. "Why, is something wrong, only it's late and...?"

He forcibly jostled me aside. "I'm sorry, but I need to come in... I need to get away from the monkeys..."

Open-mouthed, I stared out into the sheeting rain. "Monkeys? What monkeys? I don't see any monkeys."

"Well, they're there... baboons... and they're out! So you'd better get that door shut sharpish!"

I paused. "What do you mean 'out'?"

"Out runnin' round the park, that's what!"

Giving him a puzzled look, I repeated, "Running around the park?" Was he serious or what? "You'd better sit down," I told him, closing the door. "Do you want a brew?"

Nursing a mug of tea, our uninvited but clearly relieved guest began to weave his tale of how the park's baboons occasionally left their enclosure to go walkabout... and tonight was one such night.

"Their favourite 'ang-out is the cafe," he told us animatedly. "Or, should I say, the bins at the back of the cafe. Yer see, the monkeys have got a thing for dinin' out... spend hours rummaging for leftovers, then, when they've eaten their fill, start chuckin' food around." He broke into a broad grin. "So, a word of warnin', when you leave 'ere, beware of stale meat pies flyin' around, because if one of them catches yer wrong, it'll take yer bloody eye out!"

Although we laughed, we knew that a pack of rampaging baboons was far from funny – these animals were extremely dangerous.

"So, if yer don't mind," the guard added, sliding further into his chair, "I'll wait 'ere until they go back to their enclosure."

"Surely they won't go back on their own?" Carol commented.

"Yeah, they will... they don't want to miss breakfast, do they?"

"Miss breakfast?" Dan laughed.

"Yeah... the keepers arrive first thing in the morning to feed 'em, so if they don't get back quick, they'll miss out, won't they?"

What clever monkeys, I thought. Personally, I'd never ventured into the park at night – except for that one time with Smelly and Worse – and, from what I'd just heard, I was glad of it.

However, the guard's story reminded me how Vance and I had joked about our two tiny Titans getting into the lion reserve – never realising that we ourselves might have been in danger of running into a pack of marauding baboons.

Still, if that had been the case and the monkeys had decided to push their luck, I definitely knew whose side I'd choose to be on... Smelly and Worse's every time.

Crikey! Those monkeys didn't realise what a lucky escape they'd had!

55

Next morning, whilst tucking into my fry-up, I told Carla about the previous day's events – how Duchess had given me the come-on and how the monkeys liked to dine out.

Laughing, Carla told me that she'd already heard about the mischievous monkeys' nights on the town from her brother-in-law who owned one of the biggest farms in Hendle. Much of his land backed directly onto the park itself and, on the odd occasions when he'd had to call out the park keepers, they'd told him all about the monkeys' antics.

Chewing thoughtfully on a chunk of crispy bacon, I mumbled, "Call the keepers out? Why would he want to do that?"

"To catch the escaped lions, of course," she smiled.

"*Escaped lions?*" God, this was getting better and better.

Carla went on to explain that every so often a lion would breach the park's security fences and end up wandering about in one of her brother-in-law's fields.

"So what happens then?" I blurted.

"Like I said, he has to call out the keepers. Well, he can't work his land with wild lions prowling around, can he?" she finished.

"No, I suppose not. Either way, it's unbelievable. I can't see the people around here being very happy about that."

"Oh, it's all kept very hush-hush – if the locals knew there'd be a riot!" She waved a dangerous-looking fork in my direction. "And don't you go saying anything, either, or you'll get me into trouble."

"I won't say a word, Carla, honest…" I vowed solemnly. God, escaped lions… monkeys going walkabout… where would it all end?

Gobbling down the remains of my breakfast, I bid Carla a hasty farewell, jumped into my car, then sped to the dolphinarium at break-neck speed. I could hardly wait to see Dan and Carol…

"Man, if they think the monkeys are bad, wait till they get a load of the lions…!"

❦ 56 ❧

A week had passed and my enchanted mirror resembled a swamp: a deep olivine green with minimum visibility. Normally, my dolphins greeted me excitedly, but today they barely even acknowledged my presence. Only my ever-faithful Duchess ventured forward, lethargically drifting towards me before suddenly and without warning jerking back her head to throw up.

Little wonder she'd been losing her ardour this past few days – she was sick. And she wasn't the only one. The pool was littered with clouds of vomit – far too much for one dolphin. The others had been throwing up, too.

"Have you seen this, Dan? They're sick... all of them... sick! This is down to swimming in rotten, filthy water."

"Well, it's not our fault, is it?" Dan complained. "We all know whose fault it is. And, let's face it, you did warn him!"

Dan might be right, but his words gave me little comfort. I shouldn't have allowed it to get this far... should have stood up to Backhouse instead of trying to humour him. As it was, my dithering and his stubborn determination to disregard anything I might say now meant that we were looking at an emergency peak season dump – something the park owners and Head Office wouldn't tolerate. With virtually every show full to capacity, a ditch now would be deemed out of the question due to the huge amount of money involved.

Nevertheless, regardless of Company profits, with the health of my dolphins in jeopardy, I would now have no option but to force the issue with Backhouse, meaning that one of us would have to give.

And – no matter what – this time, it would not be me.

❦ 57 ❧

Open confrontation between my general manager and me was now inevitable, so it was time to box clever. I had to think of a way to bypass Backhouse and get the vets onside because without *their* backing, the pool dump would be a non-starter. It was going to be tricky because, no matter how caring the vets might be, they still wouldn't want to risk jeopardizing their lucrative Company contracts by making waves. Unfortunately, this meant that I would again have to employ stealth.

Therefore, instead of following procedure and going through Backhouse to request a veterinary visit, I telephoned Philips's assistant, Tony Forrester, personally – a strategy designed to side-step my general manager's overall authority.

Backhouse might run the dolphinariums, but I ran the dolphins, and I wasn't prepared to risk their health any longer just to placate him.

When I eventually told Backhouse what I'd done, his face turned ashen – whether due to rage or panic, I couldn't tell. Either way, he knew all too well what the ramifications of my insurgence might be. Yet, amazingly, he still clung to the belief that we might be able to avoid a total pool dump. Even then, he wasn't prepared to capitulate, so my only hope of securing the required ditch truly lay with Forrester. Head Office would only grant permission on his recommendation.

Without him, I could do nothing.

❧ 58 ❧

All next day, my dolphins struggled to perform, yet – despite the deplorable conditions – they still managed to put on an acceptable show – something a desperate Backhouse was quick to pick up on. "See, they're working fine now. I don't see a problem…"

Don't see a problem…? I'd literally pulled every trick in the book to keep Duchess and Herb'e working, yet this self-proclaimed dolphin expert didn't see a problem, once again demonstrating his profound ignorance. He literally hadn't got a clue.

"I warned you what would happen, Tommy. Time and time again, I tried to warn you – but you just wouldn't listen, would you? And if our general manager can't see what's so glaringly obvious to the rest of us, then we're all up shit creek without a paddle…"

Clearly, my words struck home. Feigning vulnerability, he wheedled, "We'll get by, Dave, if we all pull together… I'm sure we'll get by…"

I'd heard that line so many times before and didn't intend to fall for it again. Backhouse was grasping at straws.

That evening, Tony Forrester arrived as promised. After examining my dolphins, he took blood samples, then administered shots of multivitamins – all under the watchful gaze of a clearly anxious Backhouse. When he'd finished, I pulled him to one side to drive home my concerns about the effect the water was having on my dolphins' health.

"Look, Tony, you can see for yourself what a state they're in. Just look at their eyes, for God's sake – they're practically glued shut. And, if that's not bad enough, look at their skin – it's literally peeling off their bodies." A sigh of exasperation. "If it's doing that on the outside, what's it doing on the inside?"

Forrester nodded nervously, taking care not to pass comment.

"Whether you want to admit it or not," I persisted, "my dolphins are burning up in their own waste… and Backhouse is still refusing to let me pull the plug."

As feared, Forrester vacillated, reluctant to involve himself in what he deemed to be dolphinarium politics. But I had no intention of letting him off the hook: I simply pushed even harder.

"Now look, Tony, you're not gonna like this, but I have to tell you that I fully intend to log this conversation in the ledgers. So, if anything happens to one of my dolphins, it'll be down to you – not me – because I'll be covered."

He didn't reply, but from the fraught look on his face, I could tell that he didn't appreciate being blackmailed. Nevertheless, he'd got my message – in spades – and minutes later, he was heading into the auditorium to speak to Backhouse. I watched them from the far side of the pool and, although well out of earshot, gleaned all I needed to know from my general manager's body language.

As expected, next morning, a glum-faced Backhouse informed me that all the dolphins' bloods were showing abnormalities so, on Forrester's recommendation, a disgruntled Head Office had no option but to authorise a complete ditching of the pool.

Hallelujah!

Finally, I'd got my way – at long last we were officially pulling the plug on Hendle.

Fantastic! Absolutely fantastic!

I was utterly made-up – although, needless to say, Backhouse didn't share my euphoria. He silently and dejectedly retreated to his office to lick his wounds. For him, this was the ultimate humiliation. And his pain wouldn't end there, because he'd have a lot of explaining to do to Rogers and Co as to just how he'd managed to get it all so wrong.

I was well aware that my underhand tactics wouldn't win me any friends, but I didn't care. I was no longer trying to keep a foot in two camps. Regardless of whom I upset, from now on, my only allegiance would be to my dolphins. They and *only* they mattered – a stance that would put me firmly in the firing line.

It was going to take nearly forty-eight hours to dump and refill the pool, which would mean another two full days without sleep – plenty of time to write up the dolphin logs and reflect on the ramifications of my revolt.

With much satisfaction and not a little apprehension, I wrote: *"30th July 1973, At long last we are ditching the pool water at Hendle dolphinarium after having at last gained consent by the Management."*

Maybe I should have added, *"… albeit very reluctantly"*.

❧ 59 ❧

Following the pool ditch, the water took a full week to settle, but the results were apparent for all to see. Long gone were the tight-shut eyes, peeling skins and clouds of vomit. I now had four wide-eyed, mischievous dolphins, who demonstrated their delight by leaping about in joyous abandonment.

They were literally bubbling, brimming with enthusiasm. And the feeling was mutual. I'd at last won back my enchanted mirror – a crystal plane, bathed in sunlight and spitting fire. With care, this pristine water would last for at least another six to eight months before the cycle of confrontation and secret ditches started up again.

The next two months rolled blissfully by, mainly thanks to Backhouse being forced to spend most of his time at the troubled Welby. His absence meant that I was again in charge of the dolphinarium, which enabled me to concentrate on Duchess and Herb'e's forward somersault. Even so, progress was painfully slow – non-existent, in fact.

My only success over this period was with Baby and Scouse, as they continued to add more and more tricks to their show routine. In fact, the only blip in their training arose with the beaching: Baby was still reluctant to get involved. Scouse, however, improved with every session – unexpected considering his handicap. The terrible injuries he'd sustained during that botched transport from the States might easily have finished off a lesser dolphin, yet here he was embracing life with renewed vigour. It was as if his blindness had triggered an evolution – a heightening of his senses. To my mind, he was visibly evolving –

climbing to a higher level – and, in his boundless enthusiasm, he was taking me with him.

I was developing an ever-sharper psychic link with my blind dolphin. His mental transmissions were clear and precise and, on closing my eyes, I could literally feel him – even the texture of his skin – as if a mind-wave of great intimacy had washed over his battle-hardened body.

When he opened the doors to my subconscious, he exhibited none of the emotional complications that came with Duchess and Herb'e. His *connection* was truly diamond-tipped – especially during beaching training.

Beaching was a particularly strenuous trick, which Scouse embraced with great zest – a willing state of mind sadly lacking in my other three charges. He relished working within our one-to-one magic bubble, clearly viewing it as something far more important than the simple training of a trick. I got the odd feeling that he experienced our close *connection* as a light manifestation, almost as if my body radiated an aura that he could actually *see*, allowing him to escape his prison of perpetual darkness.

Although my little prizefighter's needs might sound complex, once analysed, they were in fact very simple.

Right from the start, I'd known that Scouse was somehow different. Firstly, he'd always been a loner, only appearing to feel at ease with Baby. He didn't seem to like the other dolphins, nor did he like to be touched. Even during our playtime swims, it would take only a fleeting brush against my skin for the shock of bodily contact to send him shooting off to safety. Yet, during the training of the beaching, he would actually allow me to physically manhandle him, as I pushed him off the stage and back into the water.

The only reason I could conjure for this was that, during training, my mind was constantly 'in the zone', transmitting repeated images, which he could pick up. Conversely, when relaxing in the water for playtime, my mind was at rest, breaking the psychic *connection* and condemning Scouse back to the dark.

He was certainly an enigma, yet working him was like a breath of fresh air. I loved it!

We were now very near to achieving the beaching trick. Scouse was almost there, but Baby's constant demands on his attention thwarted him at every turn. So, if we were going to stand any chance of nailing this trick, we needed to find a distraction for Baby.

Da-daa! Enter Dan…

… his job now was to keep the infant dolphin amused… amused and out of our way.

❧ 60 ❧

I mentally hold Scouse to attention. His head rocks from side to side, as if searching for sound vibrations – a behaviour I've noticed when watching blind performers such as Stevie Wonder and Ray Charles.

I memorise his image: every contour of his body, every shadow on his face, every anomaly of his battle-scarred skin. His portrait is incredible – sharp and clear.

Now I have his image, I suspend all visual contact. I must not look at him again or the spell will be broken.

Now, I begin the merge…

Concentrate, Capello, concentrate… focus on that patch of water just behind Scouse's head. Keep him out of eyeshot… whatever you do, you must not look at him… concentrate only on the water and give the mirror time to work its magic…

That's it… centre your vision on the mirror's plane… activate your inner eye. Good… good… keep concentrating… the merge is almost complete…

"Got it! We're together!"

… we are one.

It's amazing – I am actually sharing his senses, feeling his feelings… even the rhythm of my breathing matches his… shallow… slow…

"Right, lad, let's do this…"

Scouse remains perfectly still, like a statue… waiting… his body still wrapped in my mind as I mentally gauge his weight.

Pressure building...

... behind my eyes...

... back of head...

"Now Scouse, can you see? Can you see the picture?"

His head doesn't move... not an inch... not even the slightest tremor.

"I can see."

"Is everything okay, Scouse?"

Still, no movement.

"It's okay."

My mind physically tightens its grasp...

"Gosh, you weigh a ton, Scouse!"

The pressure in my head increases as I prepare for the lift. I need all my concentration, all my inner strength...

Steady... steady... a huge effort and I heave him upwards...

"Come on, Scouse! Come on – we can do it!"

I hold my breath, not daring to exhale...

Pain... pain... a dull pain behind my eyes...

A three-second delay... then I feel the surge of his powerful tail as he propels himself fully from the water, sliding onto the stage to lie by my side.

I do not physically touch him...

I do not look at him...

I *dare* not look at him...

I am aware of his presence beside me, yet, at the same time, I seem to watch us from afar...

... I see what he sees: the shared vision of a boy and a dolphin...

... I do not move...

... I do not breathe...

... I mentally hold him...

Pain... that dull pain... pushing... pushing...

"Stay! Stay! Tail up... lift your tail!"

He's fighting me... he wants to return to the water, but I can't allow it...

"Not yet, Scouse... not yet! We've got to lift your tail!"

Pressure growing… black spots exploding behind my eyes… the vision is crumbling… can't hold him for much longer…

"Lift it, Scouse… lift your tail!"

A moment's delay, then Scouse is arching his back, flexing his muscles, hauling his magnificent tail from the water…

"Yes… perfect! Hold… hold… hold…"

Keep the picture, Capello, whatever you do, don't lose the picture!

Three seconds – just three short seconds – before the shriek of my whistle shatters the vision…

… I'm solo again… free…

… the merge is over…

… but our *connection* remains.

Exhaling heavily, I wrap my arms around his bulk and physically push him back into the pool.

Whistle – fish! Whistle – fish! Whistle – fish!

"Fantastic, Scouse! Absolutely fantastic! Good boy!"

Whistle – fish! Whistle – fish! Whistle – fish!

Our excitement is overwhelming…

"You like that, David, don't you? You like that! Was it right? Was it?"

He's knows very well that it was right… he's laughing… he's literally laughing his head off.

"Perfect, Scouse, just perfect – you clever, clever boy!"

Again, momentarily, I'm lost in another realm.

Dan waits, hidden somewhere in the shadows not too far away – I just don't see him.

Then, the *connection* dissipates and pressure is gone.

I've re-entered the real world. I'm back… standing on that cold, damp stage with Dan by my side…

… and he's jubilant!

"Fantastic, Dave, I never thought he'd get it… but he has!"

I have no words for Dan. All the excitement masks just how drained I feel: my head is empty; I'm dizzy and headachy; but I have what I want… I have the beaching.

My enchanted mirror has stolen yet another fragment of me. But I don't care – it's a price I gladly pay.

With this trick in their repertoire, Baby and Scouse are now second in the UK – second only to Duchess and Herb'e.

I still can't believe it! The odd couple no one rated: a blind dolphin and an infant. Incredible – just look at them now!

Good old Scouse!

Within two weeks, Scouse's solo beaching trick had been added to the show, promoting Baby and Scouse to one of Britain's top performing teams.

Their trick list read an impressive: three opening bows, handshake, tail slap (applause), retrieval of one to three rings, retrieval of hat and sunglasses, three double hurdles, three double hoops, double tail walk, singing, bottom butt, boat tow, tail football, yes thank you/no thank you, double back somersault, highball, lifebelt, toothbrush, fish hand, wave and three closing bows…

Oh, and nearly forgot… the beaching!

All these fabulous tricks from two dolphins who'd been written-off by an ignorant Management.

Baby and Scouse had so excelled themselves that I decided to give them a much-needed rest from training and focus my attention back on Duchess and Herb'e. With only five shows a day, the season was now past its height, giving me extra time in which to pursue their double forward somersault – a quest that was fast turning into obsession. Even so, try as I might, I still couldn't seem to get through to my *Perfect Pair* – this trick was proving to be a bridge too far even for them.

During these summer months, the dolphinarium would often become oppressively hot, so I'd leave the side doors open in an effort to release the heat. Inevitably, with such easy access to the pool, my morning training sessions would attract audiences from amongst the park workers. No great shakes, as I was always too absorbed in my work to take much notice of them.

However, one character was impossible to miss, mainly thanks to his striking attire: large Stetson hat and tan riding breeches neatly tucked into highly polished boots. I found his presence disconcerting as, day after day, he sat in the auditorium, dissecting my every move with piercing blue eyes. Unlike my other onlookers, he never ventured down to the poolside, choosing instead to remain aloof, as if making a conscious effort to protect his privacy. He was certainly a strange one because, even minus his outlandish regalia, he would still have generated an unnerving presence.

He'd been watching the training sessions for about a week before I finally felt compelled to ask who he was. As I approached him, he rose gingerly from his seat, and it was only then that I realised just how small in stature he actually was – slightly built and a little over five feet tall at best.

"Hi, I hope you don't mind me watching you train," he said in a soft Canadian accent. "You see, I'm a trainer, too, so I find your methods fascinating."

"A trainer?" I repeated. "What… here at the park?"

He gave me a superior smile. "I don't actually work for the park, but for the Columbia Circus organisation, which has a contractual agreement with the park for the training of its elephants."

"Elephants?" I gasped. "So you're an elephant trainer?"

The man's smile widened as he sensed my excitement. "Yeah, I work in the elephant compound on the far side of the estate." He paused. "Do you fancy dropping by one day to take a look around? I'm sure you'd find it interesting."

You bet! I'd never been up close and personal with an elephant before, so this was an invitation impossible to resist. "Fantastic, that would be fantastic! When would be convenient?"

He tipped his hat thoughtfully. "Tomorrow morning would be good…?"

"Great… tomorrow morning it is, then…"

After he'd left, I was still buzzing, so decided to wind up my training session and devise some new show rotas instead. Starting from today, the lion's share of the work would fall to Baby and Scouse as I was keen to keep Duchess and Herb'e fresh for evening somersault training. Not that I was expecting any breakthroughs, because my mind just wasn't on the job: I couldn't stop thinking about tomorrow's visit to the elephant compound.

Another adventure just around the corner – I could hardly wait!

❦ 62 ❧

It takes a full ten minutes to drive from the dolphinarium to the elephant compound and I feel like I'm entering another world.

Security clears me for admittance, then I park outside a huge expanse of land enclosed by a fifteen-foot mesh fence. As I climb from my car, I hear someone calling to me from afar.

In the distance, I spy a small herd of African elephants – plastic toys against an alien landscape. This strikes me as odd, because I've always believed that African elephants were deemed too aggressive for training. Amongst them is a huge bull, clearly noticeable by its large head and colossal ears. And by its side is the diminutive figure of the trainer, plainly recognisable by his striking Stetson hat.

I give him a wave and wait for him to come over, but he doesn't move. Instead, he beckons me in.

The paddock entrance consists of a rudimentary door cut into the mesh fencing, leaving it practically invisible to the naked eye. Following the trainer's hand directions, I prowl back and forth along the mesh wall, struggling to locate it. After what seems like an age, I embarrassedly push my way inside.

Securing the door behind me, I'm again left waiting. But, still, the trainer doesn't move… again, he beckons me on.

The idea of walking unaccompanied across an unfamiliar paddock is unnerving. Even from this distance, the elephants look colossal. However, I don't wish to appear weak – after all, I've got my street cred to think of – so I take a deep breath, then stride purposefully forward.

Strange, I hadn't reckoned on the size of the elephant compound. It's immense... I mean, positively enormous and, as I cross its dusty plane, I find myself swallowing a little harder.

"Is it getting hot around here or is it just me?"

I can feel myself breaking into a sweat and my mouth has gone terribly dry.

"Keep going, Capello. Nothing to worry about... after all, he wouldn't have called you in here if the elephants were dangerous, would he?"

A rivulet of sweat trickling down my temple.

"God, the size of this place... a bloke could get lost in here!"

A gulp of hot air.

"Spots before your eyes... that's all you need. Still, nearly there... not far to go now. After all, when you started out, that little sod in the big hat was only a dot on the landscape... and now the little sod's a *middle-sized* dot on the landscape..."

Glaring at him through narrowed eyes.

"Who needs this? I mean, really, *who needs this?* Now you know how the Christians felt just before they got thrown to the lions."

Still no words of comfort from afar.

"What's up with the little bastard, anyway? Why doesn't he open his mouth? Has he lost his tongue, or what?"

Another gulp of hot air.

"Come on, my son, get a hold of yourself... for God's sake, stay cool..."

I note that both trainer and elephant are watching my progress with expressions of smug expectancy, as if they're enjoying the spectacle.

"Why? What do they think I'm gonna do? Run?"

At long last, I'm approaching the centre of the paddock and can see the big bull clearly. It's huge... absolutely huge... and it's looking at me funny.

"Why's it looking at me like that? Maybe it thinks I shouldn't be here...? Maybe it's right..."

Suddenly, its huge head starts swaying from side to side.

"God, what's it doing now?"

It throws back its trunk and starts to trumpet loudly.

"That's not a good sign… that's definitely not a good sign… I just know that's *not* a good sign…"

Legs frozen… heart thumping…

"Oh, shit, the bloody thing's gonna charge… it's gonna *charge*…"

All my instincts screaming… run… RUN… but I'm in the middle of the paddock… the point of no return… I'd never reach the exit in time… even assuming I could find it. In other words…

"… I've had it… I'm snookered… and, what's more, that bloody elephant knows it!"

The colossal beast starts to thunder towards me like a runaway freight train…

"Oh, shit, it's charging… the soddin' thing's charging!"

I can literally feel the ground shuddering beneath my feet. And that's not all − the scream of its challenge is deafening. I'm rooted to the spot… too terrified to even move…

"What're you gonna do, Capello… come on, get a grip, what're you gonna do?"

The beast thunders on… less than twenty feet away and still coming…

"No use bloody running now… you've left it too late… besides, there's nowhere to run to…"

Gritting teeth… clenching fists…

"Stay calm, Capello, stay calm… whatever you do, you've got to stay calm! It'll stop… it's bound to stop… it's bloody well *got* to stop…"

Ten feet away − ten short feet − and, still, the juggernaut thunders on…

"I don't think it's gonna stop… the bloody thing's *not* gonna *stop*…

"Oh, shit… shit… shit… shit…"

Suddenly, the elephant jams on the brakes, skidding to a halt less than five feet from my face.

"*God…!*"

The bloody thing's huge… it's ginormous…

I don't do anything… *can't* do anything, but suck on the dust billowing around me.

The colossus towers over me, blotting out the sunlight.

Never seen anything so big in my life... and I swear the soddin' thing's still growing!

Its breath hits me like an explosion as it trumpets in my face at full volume.

Shit... shit... shit... shit... shit... shit...

Adrenaline levels surge and a pounding heart pumps blood at lightning speed... then, my mind transmits a single thought:

"You big lummox... I know your game!"

My muscles unlock, allowing me one firm, decisive stride forward... a step into the unknown...

The huge animal falls silent, eyeing me warily, suddenly unsure.

"Not such a tough guy now, are ya, yer big bully?"

I sense its indecision and my confidence rockets. I must not allow it time to think. I take a vital second stride. Lifting my arms, I push my full body weight against the base of its trunk. "Back!" I command, "I said, *get back!*"

My voice is loud and strong and the giant begrudgingly responds. Backing away, it turns, crestfallen, to make its way back to its keeper.

Heart still threatening to explode, I press my newfound advantage by taking hold of its ear to walk alongside it. Sun-blocked beneath its huge shadow, I clock its trainer's wry smile.

"Everything okay?" he asks.

I smile through gritted teeth. "Yeah... why shouldn't it be?"

Smarmy, short-arsed little swine!

With an ill-concealed smirk, he jerks his head towards the eight-strong herd standing close by.

Panic rapidly subsiding, I follow him into their midst, where he introduces me to each individual elephant, lovingly speaking their names and stroking their cheeks.

I feel my anger slip away as I bask in their radiance. It feels both exhilarating and humbling to be so near to such magnificent creatures; to have them gently touch my face and body with their long inquisitive trunks.

Then, introductions over, the trainer takes me further into the paddock. That's when I notice a baby elephant, penned off from the others and watching us through the mesh with sad, confused eyes.

"What's up with him?" I ask. "Why isn't he with the herd?"

"There's something wrong with him," the trainer replies. "For some reason, the others won't accept him, so we've had to separate him for his own safety."

I feel a strike of pain as I spy four bloodied holes gaping in his ears. "Did the other elephants do that to him?"

"Yeah… and, if they get chance, they'll probably try to kill him. Still, not to worry, he'll be out of here soon – the park management is sending him to Kiddies' Kreche, not far from you."

Kiddies' Kreche is a small enclosure situated next to the dolphinarium, filled with petting animals like goats, llamas and rabbits – but nothing nearly so exotic as an elephant.

"Well, if he's going to be my neighbour, I'll make sure to drop in on him every morning. What's his name?"

"Captain, he's called Captain. But don't get too attached…baby elephants don't last long on their own."

"How do you mean?"

"Well, they need to be with a family – it's very important to them – and this poor little guy hasn't got one." He stares blankly at the infant for several seconds, before dismissively turning back to the herd. "Well, I'm busy… got things to do…"

Hardly subtle, but a clear signal that my audience is over.

I thank the trainer, then set off back to my car, leaving the sad-eyed Captain staring after me through the mesh.

That trainer – gosh, what a weirdo! I have no doubt that that insecure little man set me up for a fall today, hoping to bring me down a peg. Well, things didn't go quite to plan, because I like to think I passed his test with flying colours. I can't help smiling to myself…

Somehow, I don't think he'll be visiting me again.

❦ 63 ❧

Over breakfast, I recounted my elephant adventure to Carla and her boys, relaying every detail in glorious Technicolor. I especially took great pleasure in denigrating the eccentric trainer who had tried to set me up.

As promised, baby Captain did indeed end up in Kiddies' Kreche, where he relished the loving attentions of kids and parents alike. For a short while at least, this lonely little elephant had found a bit of happiness. As for me, I kept my part of the bargain by visiting him every morning before the start of training.

It was during one of these early morning training sessions that Backhouse finally arrived back from Welby. Within minutes of walking through the door, he'd summoned me to his office to deliver some shattering news.

"I don't know if you're aware, but the West Coast show has now irretrievably crashed. Therefore, Head Office is sending Baby and Scouse there to take over as lead team."

I stared at him numbly. "Lead team? What are you talking about, lead team? Baby and Scouse have special needs. You can't send them to that bloody place. Who's gonna take care of them? They belong here with me."

Backhouse fixed his eyes on the desk. "I'm not happy about it, either, but it's out of my hands. Perhaps if you'd helped out when asked, it would never have come to this. As it is, the majority of shows at West Coast are now being cancelled. It's costing the Company a fortune and Head Office just won't tolerate it."

"What about Hendle?" I yelled. "Duchess and Herb'e can't carry all the shows alone. We need a backup team... *we* need Baby and Scouse!"

Backhouse raised his eyes. "We have no choice. Hendle has two working shows. West Coast has none."

His words struck deeply, because I knew that transferring Baby and Scouse to the stricken pool was indeed the logical thing to do. Nevertheless, I felt betrayed and angry – a volcano ready to blow.

"No... they can't do this... *you* can't do this! What about all the years I've spent training them? Baby and Scouse are mine... they're *mine!*" Realising I was shouting, I took a deep breath and tried to calm myself. "Tommy, this is wrong... all wrong, especially as the situation at West Coast could have been avoided. How many times did I tell you that every pool needs a trainer?"

Backhouse stared blankly into space, refusing to answer. But I couldn't leave it there... I just couldn't! Leaning towards him menacingly, I added, "So, let me get this straight: *you're* telling *me* that *I'm* about to lose one of the best teams in the country all because of an insane Company policy... a policy that *you* introduced?"

A prickly silence continued for several moments before Backhouse saw fit to reply. "*You're* not here to question Company policy; *you're* here to do your job... so just listen. Head Office knows that Hendle needs two dolphin teams. Therefore, two untrained dolphins from West Coast will be arriving shortly to serve as replacements for Baby and Scouse. It's nearly end of season, so you should have plenty of time to train them up."

"Train them up?" I swallowed hard. "Hold on... hold on...! God, I don't believe this... what a nerve! You're telling me that the men in suits are effectively stealing over two and a half years of dedicated training, only to replace it with a load more. Well, no way... they can get lost... in fact, you can *all* get lost! I'm fed up with copping the flak for *your* bloody cockups!" I took a breath. "Anyway, aren't you forgetting something – something important? I'm not a trainer anymore... I'm a *presenter*... Remember?"

Not for the first time, I banged out of his office, slamming the door behind me. Backhouse couldn't begin to understand how I was feeling... I literally wanted to scream. I was about to lose two of my best friends and, as always, I was powerless to stop it.

Again, I'd been screwed, utterly screwed, by people who didn't give a toss... but never before like this... never like this.

❦ 64 ❧

For the first time in nearly two years, we had the dolphinarium running on an even keel, so the impending loss of Baby and Scouse didn't go down well with anyone. Not only would we lose years of work, but also we'd effectively have to start afresh with the new dolphins from West Coast – dolphins most probably barely out of the retrieval stage.

This news had a devastating effect on staff morale: one presenter resigned immediately and our fearless penguin keeper followed suit only a few days later.

I found Beryl's resignation particularly upsetting, as her dry Scouse humour had helped me through many a hard time. She felt guilty, she said, about letting me down, because she couldn't help but remember the happier times; but Backhouse's arrival had changed all that, leaving her with little option but to quit.

Even though the end of the season was approaching, the loss of two staff members would drastically increase the workload on those remaining, and the Company, ever eager to save money, would be in no hurry to replace them.

My stress levels were again shooting through the roof with only the quiet support of Dan and Carol to keep me stable. There was no doubt that I would need all their help to get through the coming weeks.

In an effort to mitigate the hurt I was feeling over Baby and Scouse, I concentrated all my energies on pursuing the forward somersault with Duchess and Herb'e – although my tortured state of mind hampered any meaningful progress. My only moments of respite were my morning visits to my little elephant friend, Captain, who always managed to raise my spirits with his affectionate greetings.

But time waits for no one, as they say, and in the twinkling of an eye, the dreaded day of Baby and Scouse's transport had dawned, meaning it was time to say goodbye to my two cherished friends – something that left me feeling utterly devastated.

Only then did I realise that my Valium wasn't working anymore.

65

I have to carry out the transport alone as there are only three presenters left to run the dolphinarium and the Company is still demanding two shows a day. As always, the men in suits want their pound of flesh...

... they make me sick... sick to my stomach.

Due to his record of fighting, Scouse is sedated for the move – always hazardous. But we dare not risk further injury; after all, the transport from America cost him dearly...

... it cost him his eyes.

The morning has a surreal feel as I catch and harness my two dolphins with cold efficiency. I have purposely imposed a psychic block on Baby and Scouse, as the last thing I need right now is to feel the warmth of their *connection*.

That would be far too painful.

There is virtual silence as we load them into the transport van. The air is dead. It's like being at a funeral: numbing, except for that sickly empty feeling in the pit of my stomach.

I feel like screaming.

Trapped in a bubble of despair, I hear the engine growling into life. Within minutes, we're on the dual carriageway heading for West Coast, a subdued Backhouse following behind in the comfort of Philip's car. The journey I've been dreading has started and I'm powerless to stop it.

In less than two hours, we will reach our destination.

In less than two hours, they'll be gone.

I'm battling to prevent feelings of utter hopelessness from morphing into raw, uncontrollable rage. My head swims with the distant echoes of my last conversation with Clive Rothwell, the West Coast manger. How I strived to explain the differences between a trainer and a presenter – a lesson I believe he's chosen to ignore.

The mere thought of leaving Baby and Scouse alone at West Coast claws at my very insides.

I'm bleeding...

... I'm hurting...

... I want to lash out...

... but I need a target... who...?

... who?

People... I hate them... hate them all.

But regardless of my pain, the clock keeps ticking and I can do nothing to slow it.

Inevitably, the van begins to crawl.

There are no windows, but I hear the ring of money from a passing amusement arcade, along with the raucous laughter and rabid chattering of attention-seeking idiots. We're near... only minutes away from our destination.

A few more swinging turns, then the van's heartbeat shudders to a halt.

Both Baby and Scouse lie quietly in their harnesses. They haven't moved a muscle throughout the entire journey.

Do they know?

Either way, I can't feel them, which means at least my psychic block is holding.

I hear car doors slamming and the murmur of distant voices. I don't move, but gaze down at my two charges in silence.

How can they do this to us?

How can they?

How *dare* they?

With each yank of the chain, the roller-shutter door of the dolphinarium assaults my ears with a torturous squeal.

Outside, I know that people are waiting, eager for me to open the van doors...

... well, let them wait...

... let them all wait.

Someone bangs on the side of the vehicle – a signal for me to open up...

... so I let them wait a little longer.

I'll open the doors when I'm good and ready... and not before.

Time passes.

I become aware that the crowd outside has fallen silent. They're anxious... they're confused.

Good... let them wait a little longer...

... let them worry.

I need time to get myself together...

... time to armour my breaking heart.

How dare they do this to us...?

... HOW DARE THEY?

The fingers of the clock freeze...

... wait... wait...

Am I ready?

No... I'll never be ready...

... NEVER!

Time...

... time to open up.

Sunlight streams into the back of the van, sunlight so bright it blinds me. I sense a crowd of sulphurous figures.

My eyes adjust.

Ah, there they are! Faces: a dozen or so anxious, twisted faces, all smiling nervously up at me.

I don't smile... I have no reason to smile.

People... I HATE THEM!

Clive Rothwell pushes to the front of the crowd. "Great to see you, David – hope there weren't any problems?"

He awaits my reply.

I don't answer.

He puts out his hand to greet me.

I don't take it.

Instead, I purposely avoid his stare and bark orders over his head, tersely instructing his undeserving staff. "Carry them with care!"

Once inside the dolphinarium, Philip gives Baby and Scouse the mandatory check, then looks at me uncomfortably.

He knows how I'm feeling.

"They're okay, David... let's get them in."

Five minutes later, it's all over. Baby and Scouse are swimming away...

... swimming into my past.

It's official. I've lost them...

... lost them forever.

I glance at Backhouse, but he furtively avoids my gaze.

I feel like ripping his head off...

Even Philip doesn't speak. He and Backhouse have obviously been talking as they followed the transport, both agreeing that today silence is the better part of valour.

I turn to a sheepish Clive. He knows what's coming, but I don't care. I'm about to throw all the bridge building from my last visit right back in his face.

I feel like a volcano about to erupt... pressure building.

Everything bottled up inside, I give... I give tenfold. It's time someone told him a few home truths about his poxy dolphinarium.

Clive doesn't like it – doesn't like the way I'm snarling at him – after all, he's the manger, a Company executive. Well, tough...

... he's not supposed to like it, so I snarl at him some more.

Just one word... if he says just one wrong word, he's had it...

... I swear, he's had it!

He says nothing.

The red mist begins to dissipate and, somewhere in the background, I hear Backhouse smarmily apologising for my behaviour.

He can apologise all he likes. I don't care anymore...

... bastards... all of them... BASTARDS!

I turn to the West Coast staff shouting, "Get your dolphins into the van! I haven't got all day... I need to get away from this shithole!"

Nobody questions me.
Nobody challenges me.
Just silent compliance.
As I leave, I don't look back...
... daren't look back.
Baby and Scouse are gone...
... gone forever.
I just want to go home... just want to get back to Hendle.

❧ 66 ❧

No matter how many pills I popped, the loss of my tiny duo continued to tear through me like a scream and although my Valium-enforced keep succeeded in deflecting Baby's song, it proved nowhere near as effective when it came down to dealing with Scouse. My blind dolphin's diamond-tipped *connection* pierced my makeshift defences like a thunderbolt from Olympus, his primal lament tormenting me constantly, calling... calling...

"David, where are you? Where have you gone? Why have you deserted me?"

"You've got to stop this, Scouse... you've got to let me go..."

I couldn't bear to listen – Scouse's melancholy cries were laced with accusations of betrayal, punishing messages constantly replaying in the darkest crevices of my mind.

"Please... David... where are you? Where have you gone?"

"I can't listen, Scouse... I WON'T listen... you've got to stop... why won't you stop?"

As Scouse grew ever more desperate to make contact, he upped the intensity of his psychic bombardment, driving me even deeper into my Valium pit.

"Please, Scouse, please... let me go... just let me go..."

For a further ten days, his frantic calls continued to plague me. Then, when on the verge of a complete mental shutdown, I awoke one morning to find him suddenly gone.

My little prizefighter had disconnected the 'phone.

Only when finding myself wrapped within this eerily muted bubble did I realise that Scouse was not the only one pulling a disappearing act: Duchess and Herb'e's song was melting away, too. The Valium shield I had so enthusiastically adopted to blot out my despair was also having an adverse effect on the psychic link to my *Perfect Pair*. This was particularly evident with Herb'e, whose *connection* was fast slipping into memory. Only my precious Duchess remained tuned-in, although even her voice had faded into a distant echo.

Muddled, befuddled and guilt-ridden, I continued to spiral from grace, slowly drifting deeper and deeper into the Valium-induced limbo I had created for myself, unwilling and unable to find my way home.

But the sanctuary I sought in the haze came at a price: silence, a deafening silence.

For the first time in my life, I felt truly alone.

❦ 67 ❧

Try as I might, I just couldn't bring myself to give the proper training time to the new dolphins. That deep feeling of anger and betrayal still raged within and, even though the fault wasn't theirs, to me, they symbolized the Company's treachery.

Instead, I spent nearly all of my time with Duchess and Herb'e in pursuit of the forward somersault. Yet, no matter how hard I tried, my efforts always ended in failure, leaving me ever more tired, despondent and frustrated.

As these failures played on my mind, I became suddenly and acutely aware of time. I felt as if the hourglass had turned, its precious sands running away, making the pursuit of this trick all consuming. For me, my dream of the forward somersault had turned into a sickness...

... I had to have it – no matter what the cost – I had to have it.

On a happier note, Backhouse was now spending most of his time at Welby. On a not-so-happy note, in an attempt to save money, he hadn't bothered to replace the staff we'd lost. This meant that those remaining had to take on extra cleaning responsibilities: auditorium, public toilets and, of course, the ubiquitous contributions of Smelly and Worse.

This didn't go down well with our last remaining girl presenter, who was quick to remind me that she hadn't applied to be a toilet cleaner and certainly didn't intend to become one. So this meant that we were now down to three – Carol, Dan and me.

Coupled with the loss of Baby and Scouse, this added pressure began to take its toll. Even so, I had to keep my chin up, as I had no intention of allowing myself to fall further into the Valium smog – the binges had to stop and stop now.

This was going to be a hard winter – in more ways than one.

ᘒ 68 ᘓ

Dan and Carol had gone home early, so for the first time in ages, I was free to train without an audience.

"Hello people, here we go again – time for another fish bonanza!"

My enchanted mirror revealed two double-chinned dolphins bobbing at the foot of the stage, Herb'e – as always – laughing in gleeful anticipation of the feast to come. Duchess, however, wasn't sharing in his euphoria. Our lack of achievement had this sensitive dolphin troubled.

For the ever-mischievous Herb'e, there were no such misgivings, as working the somersault scam presented multiple opportunities for him to take advantage. Even so, I was convinced that Herb'e held the key to this trick as, with fewer hormones flying around, his *connection* was altogether sharper than that of his partner.

As for me, I still couldn't understand why I wasn't getting through to them. I hadn't changed my method of thought training; I was still creating mind pictures; and, since cutting back on my Valium intake, our psychic link was getting stronger by the day. So what was wrong?

Perhaps I still bore a mental signature from Clyde – a psychic brand that, in all probability, would never fade. Or could it be the relentless pressure of my on-going feud with Backhouse...? A feud I knew to be grinding me down. Or even the highly distressing commandeering of Baby and Scouse...? A blow that would forever torment me. I just didn't know, but, all in all, I would be the first to admit that my recent history didn't provide the greatest CV for training Europe's only double forward somersault.

Nevertheless, despite all the doubts and negatives plaguing me, I was determined to soldier on. The time had come to let go of the past and get my dream back on track.

It was once again time to get up close and personal.

❧ 69 ❧

As I kneel on the poolside, I'm so deep in thought that I can barely feel the cold striking through my bones. Instead, I'm seduced by the soft contours of Herb'e's laughing face.

"You're a comedian, Herb'e... a real comedian."

Then, I notice...

Is it my imagination or is he squinting a little?

I look closer.

I can't be sure.

Is he smiling at me... or is he smirking?

I can't be sure.

I lean a little closer.

He cockily holds his ground.

We scrutinise each other, reminiscent of two poker players over a gaming table.

There is no doubt that the radio is on – I can hear its echo – yet he isn't saying anything. But, then again, he doesn't need to – his eyes speak volumes.

"You know, don't you?"

He thinks he can hide in his silence...

...but he's wrong.

He blinks.

He thinks I haven't clocked him...

... but he's wrong there, too.

I've got him sussed.

Then I remember – he pulled something similar to this when we were working on the back somersault.

"*You clever, clever boy, Herb'e – I'd almost forgotten!*"

The volume from the radio's just gone up a notch.

It's as if we've been playing cards every night for the last six months, but instead of picking my pocket, he's been cleverly weeding my fish bucket.

God, he's bright!

"*I know you know! You have a 'tell', Herb'e, a give-away – and I've been too blind and stupid to see it. You know! She doesn't!*"

There's a static upsurge from the radio. Duchess enters the mix. I'm now in a three-way *connection* with both dolphins.

"*He knows what?*"

She's talking. He isn't. But it doesn't matter, because I *know* that he knows.

I turn my gaze to Duchess.

"*He knows about the forward somersault, that's what!*"

"*What's a forward somersault?*"

"*God, Duchess, it's what I've been trying to teach you for the last six months, that's what.*"

My eyes flick back to Herb'e.

"*You bandit – even Dick Turpin wore a mask!*"

He's smirking… yes, no doubt about it… he's definitely smirking… I clock the imp hiding in his eyes.

"*You think you're clever, don't you, Herb'e? Think you've got one over on me? Well, time to think again, 'cause there's no more free dinners for you. That's your lot!*"

He hasn't moved an inch… hasn't made a sound. He's just bobbing in the water, psyching me out. He hopes I don't know what he's been up to. Yeah… I know all right!

"*You're waiting for me to start the training session, aren't you, Herb'e?*"

Still no words – just rascally joy tugging at my ears.

"*It's okay, Herb'e, you don't have to say anything, because I know that you know. And don't try to deny it.*"

His smirk is less pronounced than it was a few minutes ago.

"Well, sunshine, there'll be no training tonight, because I'm wise to you. You're nothing but a fiddler – a fat-faced fiddler!"

A look of pure innocence.

"What, me?"

Ohh… now he's talking!

"Yes, you, fat face… you must think I'm a right pushover!"

Did he just nod his head or what…?

"What's a pushover?"

"Don't get smart, Herb'e – you know exactly what a pushover is…"

Or does he…?

Maybe it's me who's got it wrong…?

Maybe he doesn't know what I'm talking about after all…?

And maybe he didn't nod his head, either…?

I peer harder.

"Look, Herb'e, I know you've been taking me for a ride, I just know. But I've had so much on my plate lately that I haven't been reading the signs."

He opens his mouth and wobbles his pink tongue.

"What's 'taking me for a ride'? What are you talking about?"

I can't help but laugh.

"You, my son, are impossible!"

I rearrange my aching knees, then lean down to give both him and Duchess a big hug. Poor Duch – glad of the affection as always, but still doesn't understand.

But Herb'e understands… yes… Herb'e knows all right…

"I'm the problem, aren't I, people? I'd lost sight of the basics. I'd forgotten that we're supposed to be a team… and winning teams are supposed to talk."

Duchess butts in.

"Talk about what?"

I cup her face and give her a big, fat kiss on the forehead.

"Never mind, Duch, I'll tell you more later. But, the gist of the situation is, somewhere along the line, I lost the plot and lost it big-time."

I glance at Herb'e.

"Didn't I, Herb'e?"

Herb'e continues to play the silent card.

"Okay, kid, a new game in town… here's how it goes: I'm ending all

forward somersault training until you spill the beans to Duchess. So that leaves me with a redundant bucketful of fish, which your two new neighbours will love! Besides, missing a feed won't do you any harm, you're both getting fat... especially you, Herb'e!"

My disappointed rascal – realising that his fish feasts are over – swims away, followed by a perplexed Duchess.

"What's going on? Will someone just tell me what's going on?"

With the training session cancelled, I feed the penned newcomers, then release them into the main pool for the night.

As I turn out the light, I glance back at the mirror to catch Herb'e watching me from the corner of his eye.

"Yeah... you know all right, you scoundrel..."

And to think I thought I'd lost the knack... not a chance...

"You know the score, Herb'e. Now, sort it!"

❦ 70 ❧

Throughout the coming weeks, I stayed true to my word. No somersault training took place... nor would it until Herb'e shared his secret with Duchess. I instead started to work on the beaching trick – a change of direction that really ticked Herb'e off.

During these winter months, Dan did his best to raise my gloomy spirits by introducing me to a plethora of rock music. The pool's PA system thundered to the sound of Emerson, Lake and Palmer, Amon Duul II and a wacky country and western outfit called Dan Hicks and His Hot Licks – a velvet underground of rhythmic notes that would cement my love of music for an eternity.

As these super groups lifted my daily training sessions to a new level, I began to realise just how important Dan had become. Quietly taking up the mantle vacated by Vance, this gentle and unassuming man had unwittingly become the new guardian of my fragile psyche.

Sadly, it was also during this period that my love affair with Carol began to fade. My constant mood swings and confrontational behaviour had finally succeeded in forcing us apart – yet another loss to add to my ever-growing list.

Otherwise, the weeks continued to pass uneventfully, until one cold, damp morning, a visibly excited Dan suddenly lifted the mood.

"David, guess what? There's a travelling dolphin show playing Hendle tonight. How do you fancy going?"

Strange as it may seem, I'd never sat in on anyone else's show, reason being that I'd always had my own ideas and didn't want them corrupting in any way.

"Sounds good," I replied. "It'll certainly make a welcome change from this place. Besides, I'd love to see how the other half lives."

So, decision made, we shut shop early, jumped into my car and headed for Hendle. But, as usual, once we hit the city centre, my dysfunctional sense of direction kicked in.

"Dan, I haven't got a bloody clue where we are… this flippin' awful one-way system's got me boss-eyed!"

For the next hour, we continued to navigate aimlessly through the city's honeycombed traffic system, only to arrive at our destination just as the show was finishing.

"Great… nearly an hour and a half of messing about just to miss the rotten thing! I don't believe it!"

Both Dan and I watched despairingly as the exuberant crowds filed out of the converted swimming pool.

"Come on, Dave," Dan soothed. "We may as well go in and say hello. After all, it seems stupid to come all this way for nothing."

Dan was right. Why not? We had nothing to lose, so we locked up the car and made our away into the building. But, on entering the pool room, I was more than surprised to meet the concerned face of an old friend: Philip, our vet, was standing by the door staring thoughtfully down at a slowly emptying basin.

"Hello, Philip," I grinned, "what the heck are you doing here?"

We'd obviously caught him unawares, because he spun around in surprise, eyes widening and mouth falling open. "Never mind me – what about *you*? What are *you* doing here?"

Laughing, I explained how we'd wanted to sit in on the show, but had managed instead to lose ourselves in the city's streets. "That's our sad story," I concluded, "so what's yours?"

"Well, this show's moving on tonight," he explained, "so I have to be here to oversee the catch and transport of the dolphins." Drawing his gaze back to the pool, he shook his head. "But one of these animals is a real meanie. Seriously, given half a chance, he'd have you, so the only safe way to catch him is to drain the pool with him still in it."

Glancing thoughtfully back at me, he broke into a beseeching smile. "Er… David, do you think you could do me a favour and make this catch? Otherwise, I'll be stuck here till midnight waiting for the pool to drain."

I had to smile. "God, isn't life strange?" I commented. "Only fate could have delivered me here tonight."

The vet's face immediately lit up.

So it was out of the frying pan and into the fire… yet again.

❧ 71 ❧

Despite my depressed frame of mind, the thought of taking my chances against this 'meanie' dolphin excited me... really, really excited me. Perhaps a good kick up the backside was just what the doctor ordered.

However, because of the elevated risks involved, I knew that I'd need a secondary catcher on whom I could utterly rely... and that only left Dan. Luckily, poor Dan hadn't overheard my conversation with Philip, so was unaware of the dangers attached to catching this particular dolphin. And, irresponsible though it seemed, I had no intention of enlightening him – after all, there was no point in worrying him unnecessarily.

"Sorry to drag you into this, Dan, but do you think you could give me a hand? Philip needs me to catch this dolphin and you're the only one I can trust to make the secondary catch."

Not wishing to let me down, my bamboozled partner begrudgingly consented and, within minutes, we were both standing on the poolside clad in borrowed swimwear.

Then, the oddest thing happened – as I stared into the throat of our watery arena, I suddenly became aware that I was being scanned.

An invasive, dull headache started to press against the back of my eyes, leaving me nauseous and light-headed. The radio was definitely on and transmitting a silent, threatening *connection*, one which caused me to instinctively seek out its source. Amazingly, I'd unintentionally opened a psychic door to this alien dolphin.

Incredible... he'd never laid eyes on me before; yet, of all the people present, he had already identified *me* as his combatant. Another reminder, if ever I needed one, that the *connection* works both ways. My almost nonchalant ability to fall into the dolphin mind had given me away, meaning I was now dealing with an adversary who knew my battle plan.

I continued to watch apprehensively as he treated me to an aggressive display of tail slapping and head shaking. I turned to Dan. "This guy's sussed me, and he means business. We must be quick... mustn't give him time to think..."

Dan nodded nervously.

"Remember, Dan, speed is everything... try not to think..."

Poor Dan – he'd heard that remark before.

In the background, I could hear Philip muttering instructions to the show staff and, as Dan turned to listen, I took the opportunity to prepare for the catch by sliding unobtrusively into the corner of the pool...

... but what happened next was wholly unexpected.

Only seconds in the water and the dolphin bulleted towards me. However, in his eagerness to ram me, he caught me off-centre, glancing off my side, spinning me like a Catherine wheel and inadvertently placing me in the ideal position to make a head catch.

My reaction was instinctive: falling onto him, I locked my arms around his neck, then slid down to grab his flippers and embark on a vigorous wrestling match.

The speed of events hadn't just taken me by surprise, but everyone else as well. On hearing the commotion, the poolside team turned, only to stand watching us with jaws drooping like trapdoors. Even Dan was shocked into a momentary immobility before leaping headlong into the pool to make the secondary catch.

Moments later, the astounded show staff watched in disbelief as Dan and I swam our furious captive into the poolside to harness him at super speed.

Wow... did we look good!

Our shell-shocked audience gaped in admiration, believing what they'd witnessed to be a brilliant manoeuvre planned with military precision. Yet the truth was so different – it was nothing more than a glorious blunder. They had no idea how luck had favoured me. It hadn't been a question of *me* not giving the *dolphin* time to think, but quite the opposite: the dolphin hadn't given *me* time to think – and only by good fortune had I prevailed.

However, for me, this catch had profound ramifications. What I found particularly disturbing was the fact that I hadn't sensed this dolphin's imminent attack. Somehow, he'd managed to keep his intention secret, effectively slipping beneath my radar. He was clearly capable of scanning me whilst at the same time preventing me from scanning him. This strongly reaffirmed my 'secret rooms' theory. I was now more convinced than ever that the dolphin mansion held numerous hidden retreats – private and impenetrable havens of the mind.

On a positive note, this new insight gave me hope in my pursuit of the forward somersault. It confirmed my belief that the key to this illusive trick lay hidden somewhere deep within one of Herb'e's psychic vaults. Now, all I had to do was unlock it.

As Dan and I made our way back to Hendle, I couldn't help replaying that magnificent catch in my mind, musing on how impressive it must have looked to Dan, Philip and the others…

Only *I* knew better… because I felt pretty sure that, should I ever have to face that dolphin again, I'd be the one to come out second best.

The fates had certainly smiled on me tonight. Only one drawback – I never got to see the show!

⟨ 72 ⟩

November drifted into December and Herb'e was still feeling bitter about the loss of his precious somersault training. He showed his displeasure by deliberately sabotaging Duchess' only solo trick – her highball – darting across her path during her run-up and disrupting her momentum so that she couldn't make the jump. There was no doubt that my rascally Herb'e was extracting every last ounce of pleasure from his childish revenge – a sobering reprisal for the loss of his fish bonanza.

Further, he constantly invaded our *connection* by generating images of the somersault – visions which he cleverly managed to conceal from Duchess. He was now openly taunting me by dangling the somersault carrot under my nose.

"Ha, ha – I know and she doesn't!"

"I don't know what?" Duchess snapped.

Crouching on the stage and smiling through gritted teeth, I tried to comfort my clearly frustrated princess.

"Ignore him, Duch, he's only trying to wind you up."

Duchess shook her head in exasperation.

"Well, he's getting on my nerves…"

I threw Herb'e a narrow-eyed glance.

"Yeah, tell me about it… he's getting on mine, too."

With my dream team at loggerheads like this, it would be impossible to resume somersault training, even if I wanted to. Much as I hated to admit it, Herb'e was now pulling the strings.

However, this unwelcome intermission finally forced me into giving some attention to the much-neglected West Coast dolphins – a female called Twinkle and a male named Eccles.

Twinkle was a seemingly untalented dolphin who'd need a lot of work. But Eccles was good – in fact, he had all the makings of being a very special performer. I remembered how excitedly Gerry had talked about him during one of his visits.

Admittedly, I didn't know much about Eccles, because he was part of Gerry's third shipment, but I did wonder if he might be the incentive I needed to develop Hendle's new team. Or maybe not – maybe I was just fooling myself, grasping at straws, because the very sight of these two unfortunate dolphins only served to remind me of the two I'd lost. Even after all this time, I still found it impossible to forgive Management's callous decision to rip away Baby and Scouse – something that would forever haunt me.

Speaking of callous Management, it was during this period that Backhouse returned from Welby – as always bearing bad news. It wasn't long before I found myself standing in his inner-sanctum listening to yet another barmy Backhouse brainwave.

"Due to the exorbitant cost of running the West Coast dolphinarium during the off-season, as from next year, all its dolphins will be transferred to Hendle for the winter."

My heart dropped like a stone. I was mortified. "Transferred *here* for the winter? Hold on a minute – whose crazy idea is this? It was bad enough when we had six dolphins, so just what am I supposed to do with eight?"

As usual, Backhouse graced me with a condescending sneer. "The decision is not up for debate; it's already been approved at the highest level."

I shook my head, sighing resignedly. "In all my time with the Company, I don't think I've ever heard anything so ridiculous or cruel. Not only is this policy totally obscene, but it just won't work."

Backhouse's response was, as ever, well prepared.

"It will work if correctly managed."

"No… no… it won't. For starters, what about the water? Our filtration system can't cope with the dolphins we've got, never mind any more. It's crazy, just crazy!"

"The water won't be a problem. Head Office has already made arrangements for a specialist team to come in and replace the filter beds."

My general manager's confident answer merely confirmed my suspicions – that this insane proposal hadn't been seeded by the Company hierarchy, but by him.

I didn't argue. Couldn't argue. In fact, I was fed up to the back teeth with arguing. Besides, there was no point – this policy was going ahead with or without my approval. Nevertheless, I found the decision galling, because it meant that Backhouse had again succeeded in manipulating the men in suits by dangling the money carrot.

For some time I'd known that my dolphins' welfare came a very poor second to Company profits, but never in my worst nightmare could I have envisaged this. This idea would entail imprisoning dolphins in seven-foot square pens for weeks – if not months – on end. An enforced incarceration that would not only damage their mental state, but also mine. Even worse, I knew all too well that Backhouse would insist on supplying some kind of limited winter show, making it impossible for me to move or free any dolphins not already in the main pool.

It was also blatantly obvious that the re-conditioned filters would prove useless with so many dolphins packed into such a small area – a mere technicality for King Tommy who knew that increased profits would discourage the Board from asking too many awkward questions.

This wintering policy would effectively turn me into a Master of Keys – more gaoler than trainer – a position that, for me, would be untenable. Yet I knew that a refusal to comply would mean losing both my job *and* my *Perfect Pair*.

It seemed that, once again, my dolphins and I were going to end up paying the price for yet another crazy Backhouse-inspired policy.

All that misery, all that torment, just to feed one man's insatiable lust for prestige and power.

And to think there was a time I used to respect him…

… used to call him friend.

Respect him?

That was a million years ago…

… now I detested him.

❦ 73 ❧

After the briefing, I left Backhouse's office feeling worn down and utterly deflated. I desperately needed to get away from the dolphinarium, so, in an effort to lift my spirits, I decided to pay a visit to my little elephant friend, Captain. But on reaching Kiddies' Kreche, I found he was nowhere to be seen. Assuming that the cold weather had kept him indoors, and still not wishing to return to the dolphinarium, I decided instead to bumble along to the restaurant for an early lunch.

With virtually no punters around at this time of year, the majority of the restaurant customers were park workers, eager to escape the cold; but, today, their usual noisy banter was noticeably absent.

Spying the face of a keeper pal, I grabbed a mug of hot tea, then shuffled towards his table. "God, what's wrong with this lot – they look like they've been to a funeral?"

On hearing my remark, the crowd fell into a stony silence.

"What's wrong?" I gasped. "What have I said?"

My friend lifted his eyes to meet mine and my heart skipped a beat. There was no mistaking his broken expression, the pain etched across his face.

"Haven't you heard? It's Captain – he's dead. Poor little fella died some time during the night. One of the lads found him early this morning."

"Captain…? Dead…?" A sickly emptiness invaded the pit of my stomach. "Oh no… no…"

I didn't say anything else – couldn't say anything else – just gazed numbly into space.

The loss of my little elephant friend was literally the last straw, thrusting me into an even deeper despair.

For me, my beloved Hendle was fast becoming a dark place, its magnificent dolphinarium morphing into a prison with invisible bars – a prison from which there seemed to be no escape. A far cry from the fairy tale world I'd envisaged when embarking on my magical career.

Now, my only desire was to be free… free of this nightmare realm. But, for me, this could never be, because of the two people I loved the most… the two people I worshipped…

… Duchess and Herb'e…

… my *Perfect Pair*…

… my gaolers.

❈ 74 ❈

A particularly hard winter left the park smothered in a blanket of white. The barren landscape was bleak and unforgiving, keeping man and beast alike indoors.

Thankfully, Backhouse spent much of his time seeking the warmer climes of Welby – a situation that suited us both. The barrier now dividing us was as icy as it was impenetrable, and I knew that it was just a matter of time before a final conflict would ensue – a conflict I couldn't possibly win.

But my woes didn't end there. Nowadays, Dan and Carol always left work early. And who could blame them? Being around me couldn't be much fun. The debilitating loss of Baby and Scouse and the sudden death of little Captain had finally pushed me over the edge – a fate I once again all too readily embraced.

The harsh winter saw me profoundly changed. With no shows, I no longer needed to dress for the public. I rarely washed or shaved, constantly stank of fish and took a perverse pleasure in wallowing in a renewed state of Valium-fuelled self-pity.

I struggled trance-like to carry on as a full month morphed by. Then, late one night, having abandoned yet another fruitless training session, I found myself stranded in the park. My car, no longer fit to withstand the atrocious winter weather, had finally given up the ghost, leaving me with no option but to set out for home on foot.

As I stumbled along the lonely road leading from the public area to the main gate, the park was veiled in darkness. A thick band of pitch obscured the moon, making it almost impossible to see, and I struggled to navigate blindly over jagged stones and protruding tree roots. Then, suddenly and unexpectedly, the weather took a turn for the worse. It began to hail stinging chips of ice that turned my flesh blue and crunched beneath my feet – an arctic onslaught coating my path in a sparkling carpet.

The road glinted with a thick layer of rough-cut diamonds, lighting a twinkling trail through the blackness. As I approached the park entrance, the path's icy finger gave way to the muted lights of the dual carriageway. Face still smarting from the hail, I stood shivering on the flooded roadside where, in desperation, I set about attempting to flag a lift – but to no avail. Who the hell would risk picking up a loser like me? Wet, bedraggled and stinking, I probably resembled a drowned rat.

With no saviour in sight, I squelched unceremoniously along the murky carriageway for another ten minutes before reaching the adjoining road. It was then that I spied the uplifting sight of a distant double-decker bus scything through the driving sleet.

Thank God – a chariot from heaven!

As I climbed aboard, trembling and fiddling in my pockets for change, the bus guard warily weighed me up. Little wonder! What a horrible, horrible mess – greasy wet hair, pale unshaven face and reeking of fish.

I forced a self-conscious smile before nervously holding out my hand with the bus fare. Having only ever travelled by car, I didn't have a clue about the cost. "How much to Hendle village?" I asked tentatively.

The guard didn't speak, but scrutinised my face and clothes, and – for a moment – I thought he was going to throw me off the bus. But, as my pleading eyes met his, his expression suddenly softened and he reached out to gently close my hand around my money.

I gave him a puzzled look. "I'm sorry, I don't understand... I..."

"Never mind the fare, lad," he said, with a sympathetic smile, "the bus company's got enough money. Go and get yourself a hot cuppa tea instead."

I stared at him, speechless, as he turned to climb the stairs to the upper deck. He was giving me a free ride and all because he'd mistaken me for a down-and-out...

… a down-and-out…! … a tramp…!

What a wake-up call!

Until that moment, I'd never realised just how low I'd actually sunk, and I decided there and then that things were going to change. I wouldn't allow myself to just roll over and die. Tonight I was going to start my fight back – beginning with a long, hot bath and a much-needed shave. Then tomorrow, I'd dump my rotten, filthy, smelly coat…

… and – more importantly – my Valium.

There would be no more fumbling through a chemical-induced fog for me. My medication was going where it should have gone a long time ago – in the bin.

Then, next job on the agenda would be a long, hard talk with Herb'e regarding a certain forward somersault.

Yeah… starting from tonight I was gonna get my life back.

On reaching my stop, I gave the guard a reassuring smile before stepping back out into the arctic gloom. Despite the hammering rain, I clearly caught the sound of his voice as the bus pulled away. "Good luck, lad!"

Then he was gone, swallowed up in time.

I stood for several moments in bewildered silence, oblivious to the hailstone stinging my cheeks. I'd just received a message, and from a man I'd known for only minutes – a uniformed angel shouldering a ticket machine.

Strange as it might seem, I couldn't even recall his face; but the one thing I knew I'd never forget was the kindness of that Hendle bus guard on such a miserable, wintry night…

"Whoever you are, wherever you are… thanks, mate!"

❧ 75 ❧

Determined to sort myself out and win back the trust of my *Perfect Pair*, I embraced the following weeks with renewed gusto – a state of euphoria no doubt boosted by my sudden realisation of just how close I'd come to pressing the self-destruct button.

However, the darkness in which I'd hidden myself for so long had left its mark. And the bottled-up anger that had driven me there in the first place remained when I re-emerged into the light, leaving me again much changed.

Mentally, I felt stronger, more self-assured – harder. It was as if I'd birthed a symbiote: a darker side that had flushed away my fairy-tale conception of the dolphin realm I thought I knew. Even more apparent, I was not alone in this transition: Duchess and Herb'e had changed, too. That bond of innocence we once shared had gone, leaving in its wake three hard-nosed professionals ready and able to face the harsh environment in which they now operated.

Gone were the rose-tinted glasses: ours was a new bond born of betrayal and fuelled by anger and – for better or for worse – there was no going back.

What struck me as particularly telling was, during my depression, I had felt abandoned and alone: yet, in truth, I couldn't have been more wrong. My *Perfect Pair* had never left me at all, but stayed by my side experiencing my ordeal. I'd been just too blind to see them, just too numb to feel them. Yet more proof that the *connection* did indeed work both ways.

So why did I keep forgetting?

Whilst I'd been floundering in the wilderness, Backhouse had wasted no time in promoting himself as the celebrity face of the dolphin project and, although he still remained answerable to Rogers, the Company seemed more than willing to hand over the reins to its new saviour – a decision evidenced by its formal acceptance of his hideous wintering policy.

Backhouse's growing popularity with the men in suits now meant that his manipulative presence cloaked all three Company pools, making it impossible for us not to clash – dangerous considering the incipient physical aggression now boiling between us.

But no matter how delightful the thought of giving my general manager a good thumping might be, it was a pleasure I'd have to put on hold as, without doubt, any fisticuffs would result in my instant dismissal.

This meant I had no choice but to again move into stealth mode. I was convinced that Backhouse and his supporters had already planned my demise from the Company and even now had my replacement waiting in the wings. Therefore, I had to show the Company hierarchy that I was still an indispensable cog in the dolphinarium machine – which wasn't going to be easy.

As far as I could see, the only way to do this was to train what had so far proved untrainable, achieve what had so far been unachievable: the double forward somersault.

Only by presenting the public with the complete shadow ballet could I scupper any plans to get rid of me, because not only would these tricks elevate Duchess and Herb'e to cult status, they'd also make me virtually untouchable. It was well known that the loyalty of my dream team stretched to no one but me.

The situation I now found myself in meant that failure was no longer an option, meaning time had again become the enemy.

I had to deliver – and I had to deliver fast. Either that or start praying for a miracle…

Little did I know, however, that the miracle was literally only two hours away. News was trickling down from the West Coast dolphinarium that since my tiny duo's enforced repatriation, things hadn't been going to plan. It seemed that the seaside venue was once again in turmoil as one-half of my stolen team had permanently downed tools – proving that unconditional loyalty wasn't just a trait of my *Perfect Pair*.

There was indeed another – one I'd tried so hard to forget…

… Scouse.

He'd stopped working…

The adventure concludes with the explosive *The Perfect Pair: Shards from the Mirror*. Coming soon!

THE PLAYERS WHO HAVE LEFT
THE STAGE

Bonnie: This fabulous dolphin and her long-term partner, Clyde, continued to wow UK audiences until she swam into the light on 12th June 1982. This gentle giant took her final bow in the same dolphinarium that she and her partner officially opened all those years ago - a prestigious event which I had the honour of hosting.

She was part of one of the finest dolphin teams ever to grace the European stage and touched the lives of all who met her. With her freedom finally won, this proud yet unassuming dolphin Queen graciously surfed the wave of tranquillity into the soft currents of Heaven's ocean... where she still swims to this very day.

Clyde: They say that time is a great healer and when trainers talk about Clyde, they do so with a genuine affection and impish delight, conveniently choosing to forget the merry dance that he led them for so long. Nevertheless, in his heyday, Clyde and his long-suffering partner, Bonnie, were without doubt the bright centre of the 1970s dolphin scene.

After Bonnie's passing, Clyde was paired with a new companion who went by the name of Sooty.

Due to the continuing practice of destroying logbooks on the death of a dolphin, we cannot verify the exact date of Clyde's final journey with any certainty. But to the best of our knowledge, he passed over on 7th December 1986.

Thus, my greatest dolphin adversary finally claimed his freedom in the calming waters of tranquillity - although, knowing him as I do, I can only surmise that Heaven's seas didn't stay tranquil for very long.

"Enjoy your retirement, you old rascal – I will never forget you!"

Captain: On a cold winter's night over forty years ago, this sad and confused little elephant closed his eyes to sleep, but never woke up. Still cradled in innocence, he drifted peacefully from dreamland into the eternal realm, where his damaged psyche was lovingly restored. Captain chose never to return to those who had shunned him, but instead found happiness playing amongst the stars as a permanent child of the universe… never again to feel unloved.

THE STORY THAT STARTED
IT ALL...

For those of you who have fallen on this book by accident, you've missed a huge chunk of the story. *The Perfect Pair: The Mirror Cracks* is in fact the second book of the dolphin trilogy, the first being *The Perfect Pair: The Enchanted Mirror*, a tale inspired by a short story written over forty years ago entitled *Deliver Us From Bobby!*

The piece about Bobby – a troubled Californian sea lion – won First Prize in the prestigious *Manchester Evening News* 'A Piece of Your Life' literary competition, and headlined in the newspaper itself on Monday 5th December 2011 as *David's Sea Lion Makes a Literary Splash*.

The judges consisted of Professor Brenda Cooper, Dr Ursula Hurley and Peter Kalu, to whom I am eternally grateful, for their choice gave me the confidence and kick-start needed for the writing of *The Perfect Pair* trilogy.

However, all too aware that I couldn't undertake this mammoth task alone, I secured the services of my sister, Tracy J Holroyd, much-published author of children's work.

So, for all those who are reading this piece for the first time, just think what you've missed.

And for the faithful preparing to read this story again, enjoy!

"Down the narrow, winding corridor, he pursued his quarry, galloping clumsily and ineffectively like... well, like a sea lion out of water."
David Holroyd
1ˢᵗ
Deliver Us From Bobby

Manchester Evening News 1971 – David lands 'a dream of a job'. My first taste of fame: I was the lucky lad chosen to represent a leading company working as a presenter of dolphin shows. Little did I realise that this opportunity would set me on the path of training The Perfect Pair – Europe's top performing dolphins. So, it seems strange that the first of my many adventures took place, not with a dolphin, but instead with a huge Californian sea lion, named Bobby.

Bobby and I met by chance after he was stealthily whisked away from his zoo home, following a horrific attack on a member of the public. To avoid destruction, he was transported to the training pool where I was based; and with nothing more than two penguins, aptly named Smelly and Worse, to keep us company, he and I soon became good friends. However, his fearsome reputation always commanded respect.

One morning, I had to pick up a crate of herring from the fishmonger's, and as the pool was situated near the local colliery, I set out early to dodge the morning traffic.

Only one road led from the village to the pit: it ran up a steep hill, passing the pool about three quarters of the way up and, thirty minutes before a shift change, got very busy.

I didn't fancy lugging heavy slabs of fish any great distance, so instead of parking in my usual place round the side of the pool, I found a more convenient spot on the main road, a short way from the front entrance.

After dumping the fish in the sink to defrost, I began to clean up the usual overnight mess left by Smelly and Worse. Filling a bucket with hot water and bleach, I strode into the pool room, calling cheerfully to Bobby, "Hello, lad, how you doing, my son?"

It was important to greet the big fellah properly: God knows, it must have been a bleak life for him locked up in this place twenty-four hours a day with nothing but two stinky penguins for company.

Bobby, messing in the water, responded to my shout by lifting his massive head, snorting a plume of droplets into the air, and solemnly regarding me with those big, green eyes. A blink of acknowledgment, then he dived to continue his sub aqua meanderings.

I picked up the deck scrubber, walked to the far end of the pool room, and started to scrub the floor. Smelly and Worse had been particularly productive overnight, leaving a fair number of stinky white pools for me to deal with.

Suddenly, the main doors to the pool room banged open, revealing a miner: early thirties, becapped and dressed in the usual drab garb of the village men.

"Hello? Can I help you?"

The doors hadn't even swung shut behind him before he started yelling abuse of the most remarkable colour. A potent Shire accent delivered four-letter words with the efficiency of a machine gun, and as I stood there gaping, I managed to grasp something about... my car... HIS space... and get it shifted NOW!

It seemed the man was aggrieved because I'd parked in *his* spot – no small offence in the village, where the ownership of a *spot* was of paramount importance. The village was so small and intimate that almost every square foot was deemed to belong to *someone:* be it a parking space, a lamppost to lean on, a wall to sit on, or a stool in the pub. I'd transgressed seriously, and the man was determined to let me know it.

Like all the miners, he was short in stature, but wide and muscular in build, with a chest that looked solid enough to stop a small nuclear warhead. He rather put me in mind of a vertically-challenged Minotaur. His small, steely eyes flashed beneath his cap, the corners of his mouth twisting grimly downwards, then he pounded towards me across the tiled floor, fists clenched.

"Are yer listenin' to mi, or what? I said, are yer listenin'?"

He was very, very angry.

But he wasn't the only one: the training pool was supposed to be a high security facility, strictly out of bounds to the public. It galled me no end that this guy had had the nerve to even breach the main entrance, never mind intrude as far as the pool room.

"Ay, you – you *******! Get that ******* car out of my space!"

Before my eyes, the red mist started to form, and I struggled to steady myself and speak calmly. "You shouldn't be in here."

"Get that ******* car out of my space!"

"Who do you think you're talking to?" I demanded, throwing the deck scrubber aside and stepping forward.

"I said get that ****** car out of my space!"

"Or what?" So enraged was I by his foul-mouthed assault, I could hardly breathe, never mind speak. Everything around me seemed to fade away as all my attention focussed on this nasty, bullish man, and my overwhelming desire to pound him into the ground. I launched myself at him, determined, dangerous and blinded by anger. He had no intention of backing off, either, and if we'd ever reached each other, I dread to think what might have happened. But we didn't reach each other, because a terrifying thought suddenly popped into my mind and all but paralysed me.

Bobby! Where's Bobby?

Distracted, I turned to see him: his massive, black head in the centre of the pool, immobile and watching. Then, ever so slowly, it swivelled round so that his big green eyes locked onto mine. For the oddest moment, it seemed as though I were looking in a mirror; then I felt all my aggression seeping away, and saw it – actually saw it – filling up in those big green eyes.

Bobby's head snapped back round to look at the man; then he dived.

There was nothing left in me now but panic, blind panic. "Run!" I screamed. "The sea lion! Run!"

The man froze in bewilderment, sensing my terror. "What? What do you mean?"

"Just get out! The sea lion!" My voice had deteriorated into a shriek.

He stood there, jaw drooping foolishly, then whimpered, "Why, does it bite?"

By this time, the torpedo which was Bobby had almost reached the deck, a plume of water in its wake.

"Go, go!" I screamed; but the man was already gone, a pair of swinging doors the only evidence that he'd ever been there.

Bobby shot from the water like a ball launched in a pinball game, a loud, hoarse bark reverberating off the walls. He hit the tiles with a dull thwack, then slid headlong through the swing doors, sending them crashing off their hinges.

As he disappeared into the dark corridor, I grabbed the deck scrubber and chased after him. "No, Bobby, no... come back!"

Down the narrow, winding corridor, he pursued his quarry, galloping clumsily and ineffectively like... well, like a sea lion out of water.

By this time, the man had made it out of the building, down the steps and onto the road, and might have believed – mistakenly – that he'd reached safety; but the avenging Bobby motored on.

"Stop, Bobby! You can't do this!"

Still bellowing his ear-shattering war cry, he burst through the main entrance, slid down the steps, and galloped along the pavement, oblivious to the crawling traffic and gaping drivers. But he managed only five or six yards before his rampaging pursuit slowed to a half-hearted slither. His prey had escaped, and Bobby just wasn't built for manoeuvring along pavements. He flopped to a stop, then lifted his head to regard me apologetically. Sorry, Dave; he got away.

By this time, the traffic had come to a complete halt as the men intended for the early shift stopped to watch. How could this be happening in a tiny, unrecognised backwater like this? A sea lion? Most of them had never seen a sea lion, except in pictures. But this? A sea lion on a road in the middle of the village?

Bobby ignored them. He was dejected, exhausted.

I blinked at him kindly, as he had so often blinked at me, then gently manoeuvred him round with the deck scrubber. "Come on, Bobby. We showed him. Now let's go home."

Bobby sighed heavily, then began the laborious journey back to the pool, hauling himself up the steps and through the entrance, still maintaining an audience of open-mouthed motorists.

As for the aggressive miner, we never saw him again.